Essential Docker for ASP.NET Core MVC

Adam Freeman

Apress®

Essential Docker for ASP.NET Core MVC

Adam Freeman
London, UK

ISBN-13 (pbk): 978-1-4842-2777-0   ISBN-13 (electronic): 978-1-4842-2778-7
DOI 10.1007/978-1-4842-2778-7

Library of Congress Control Number: 2017938878

Managing Director: Welmoed Spahr
Editorial Director: Todd Green
Acquisitions Editor: Gwenan Spearing
Development Editor: Laura Berendson
Technical Reviewer: Fabio Claudio Ferracchiati
Coordinating Editor: Mark Powers
Copy Editor: Kim Wimpsett
Compositor: SPi Global
Indexer: SPi Global
Artist: SPi Global
Cover image designed by Freepik

Distributed to the book trade worldwide by Springer Science+Business Media New York, 233 Spring Street, 6th Floor, New York, NY 10013. Phone 1-800-SPRINGER, fax (201) 348-4505, e-mail orders-ny@springer-sbm.com, or visit www.springeronline.com. Apress Media, LLC is a California LLC and the sole member (owner) is Springer Science + Business Media Finance Inc (SSBM Finance Inc). SSBM Finance Inc is a Delaware corporation.

For information on translations, please e-mail rights@apress.com, or visit http://www.apress.com/rights-permissions.

Apress titles may be purchased in bulk for academic, corporate, or promotional use. eBook versions and licenses are also available for most titles. For more information, reference our Print and eBook Bulk Sales web page at http://www.apress.com/bulk-sales.

Any source code or other supplementary material referenced by the author in this book is available to readers on GitHub via the book's product page, located at www.apress.com/9781484227770. For more detailed information, please visit http://www.apress.com/source-code.

Printed on acid-free paper

Dedicated to my lovely wife, Jacqui Griffyth.
(And also to Peanut).

Contents at a Glance

Contents

About the Author

Adam Freeman is an experienced IT professional who has held senior positions in a range of companies, most recently serving as chief technology officer and chief operating officer of a global bank. Now retired, he spends his time writing and long-distance running.

About the Technical Reviewer

Fabio Claudio Ferracchiati is a senior consultant and a senior analyst/developer using Microsoft technologies. He works for BluArancio (`www.bluarancio.com`). He is a Microsoft Certified Solution Developer for .NET, a Microsoft Certified Application Developer for .NET, a Microsoft Certified Professional, and a prolific author and technical reviewer. Over the past ten years, he's written articles for Italian and international magazines and coauthored more than ten books on a variety of computer topics.

CHAPTER 1

■ ■ ■

Understanding Docker

Docker is a set of tools for creating and running application in containers, which isolates the application from all the other software running on a server. Even though the server may be running dozens—or even hundreds—of containers, each application is shielded from all the other instances and operates as though it is the only application running.

This book explains how you can use Docker for ASP.NET Core MVC applications and how containers make it easier to develop, deploy, and manage those applications in production environments.

What Do You Need to Know?

To get the most from this book, you should be familiar with .NET Core and ASP.NET Core MVC development, including how to create, compile, and run projects in Visual Studio or Visual Studio Code. You should also have a basic familiarity with Windows, Linux, or macOS and be able to run commands using a command prompt.

What Is the Structure of This Book?

This book is split into eight chapters. Chapter 2 provides a quick reference for all the Docker commands and features described in this book so you can easily find what you need in the future without having to search through the rest of the book. Chapter 3 contains instructions for getting ready, including installing Docker, Visual Studio, or Visual Studio Code and the supporting tools that are required. Chapter 3 also includes instructions for creating a simple ASP.NET Core MVC project that is used as an example throughout the rest of the book.

Chapters 4–7 explain how to use Docker with ASP.NET Core MVC projects. Chapter 4 introduces images, which are the templates used to create containers, and shows you how to create your own images and use them to produce containers. Chapter 5 covers the Docker features for storing data and connecting the applications in different containers together. Chapter 6 describes the Docker support for describing complex applications that require different types of containers, and Chapter 7 demonstrates the Docker support for clustering servers together to run larger numbers of containers. The final chapter, Chapter 8, comes full circle and explains how the features from the rest of the book can be applied to the development environment instead of production.

Is This an Exhaustive Docker Reference?

No. This book covers the essential Docker features for working with ASP.NET Core MVC applications. I have left out Docker features that have no bearing on MVC applications or that are unlikely to be used by the majority of projects.

© Adam Freeman 2017
A. Freeman, *Essential Docker for ASP.NET Core MVC*, DOI 10.1007/978-1-4842-2778-7_1

Are There Lots of Examples?

There are *loads* of examples, and every chapter shows you how Docker works by demonstrating, not describing, the features. At the end of this book, you will have a solid understanding of what Docker does, how it does it, and why it is useful when developing and deploying ASP.NET Core MVC applications.

You can download the examples for all the chapters in this book from apress.com. The download is available without charge and includes the example ASP.NET Core MVC project and the configuration files so that you don't have to create them yourself. You don't have to download the code, but cutting and pasting the code into your own projects is the easiest way of experimenting with the examples.

THIS BOOK AND THE DOCKER RELEASE SCHEDULE

Docker is actively developed, and new releases appear often. For the most part, new releases fix bugs and add new features, but Docker is a fast-moving target, and sometimes there are breaking changes.

It doesn't seem fair or reasonable to ask you to buy a new edition of this book every few months, especially since the majority of Docker features are unlikely to change. Instead, I will post updates following the major releases to the GitHub repository for this book, for which there is a link on apress.com.

This is an experiment for me (and for Apress), and I don't yet know what form those updates may take—not least because I don't know what the future Docker will contain—but the goal is to extend the life of this book by supplementing the examples it contains.

I am not making any promises about what the updates will be like, what form they will take, or how long I produce them before folding them into a new edition of this book. Please keep an open mind and check the repository for this book when new Docker versions are released. If you have ideas about how the updates could be improved as the experiment unfolds, then e-mail me at adam@adam-freeman.com and let me know.

Which Operating Systems Are Supported?

All of the examples in this book have been tested with all three operating systems: Windows, macOS, and Linux. The exception is Chapter 7 because the Docker clustering features that it describes are supported by Docker on Linux server only.

Why Should You Care About Docker?

Docker helps to solve two important problems that affect any complex project but that are especially prevalent in ASP.NET Core projects: the consistency problem and the responsiveness problem.

What Is the Consistency Problem?

Most ASP.NET Core MVC applications are made up of multiple components. There will be at least one server running the MVC application and usually a database to persistently store data.

Complex applications may require additional components: more application servers to share the work, load balancers to distribute HTTP requests among the application servers, and data caches to improve performance. As the number of components increases, additional servers are needed, as are networks to link everything together, name servers to aid discovery, and storage arrays to provide data resilience.

Few projects can afford to provide each developer with a complete replica of the production systems. As a consequence, developers create an approximation of the production systems, typically running all the components required by an application on a single development workstation and ignoring key infrastructure such as networks and load balancers.

Working with an approximation of the production system can lead to several different difficulties, all of which arise because the platform that the developer is using is not consistent with the production systems into which the application is deployed.

The first difficulty is that differences in the environment can cause the application to behave unexpectedly when it is deployed. A project developed on Windows but deployed onto Linux servers, for example, is susceptible to differences in file systems, storage locations, and countless other features.

The second difficulty is that the approximations developers use to represent the production environment can drift apart. Dependencies on different versions of development tools, NuGet packages, and even versions of the .NET Core and ASP.NET Core runtimes can occur, leading to code that makes assumptions that are not valid in production or on other developers' workstations, which have their own approximation of production.

The third difficulty is performing the actual deployment. The differences between development and production systems require two configurations, one of which is difficult to test until the moment of deployment. I have lost track of the amount of time that I have spent over the years trying to deploy applications only to find that a single character is missing from a configuration setting or that there is a hard-coded assumption that the database can be accessed via localhost.

The fourth difficulty is that it can be difficult to ensure that all the servers for an application are configured consistently. A misconfigured server may cause only periodic problems, especially if a user's HTTP requests are distributed to a large group of servers, and identifying the problem and isolating the cause can be a difficult task, made fraught by having to perform diagnostics on a live production system.

How Does Docker Solve the Consistency Problem?

When you put an ASP.NET Core MVC application in a container—a process known as *containerization*—you create an image, which is a template for containers that includes the complete environment in which the application will exist. Everything that will be used to run the application is part of the image: the .NET Core runtime, the ASP.NET Core packages, third-party tools, configuration files, and the custom classes and Razor views that provide the application functionality.

Docker uses the image to create a container, and any container created from the same image will contain an identical instance of the ASP.NET Core MVC application.

If you adopt Docker for the development phase of your project, the developers will all use a single image to create and test the application. The development image is still an approximation of the production system, but it is a more faithful replica and will differ only by including development tools such as a compiler and a debugger. In all other regards, the development image will have the same contents as the image used to deploy the application, with the same file system, network topology, NuGet packages, and .NET runtime.

A production image is created when the application is ready to be deployed. This image is similar to the one used by the developers but omits the development tools and contains compiled versions of the C# classes. The production image is used to create all of the containers in production, which ensures that all the instances are configured consistently. And, since the development and production images contain the same content, there is no need to change configuration files in production because the database connection strings that worked in development, for example, will work in production without modification.

What Is the Responsiveness Problem?

Traditional methods for deploying ASP.NET Core MVC applications make it hard to respond to changes in workload. The approach of deploying an application to Internet Information Services (IIS) running on Windows Server means that adding capacity is a substantial task, requiring additional hardware and configuration changes to add servers to the environment.

The overhead required to increase capacity makes it difficult to scale up an application to short-term surges in demand, and the process of decommissioning capacity makes it difficult to scale down an application once peak demand has passed. The result is that ASP.NET applications have historically struggled to provision just the right amount of capacity to deal with their workload, either suffering from too little capacity at peak times (which affects user experience) or too much capacity outside of the peaks (which drives up the cost of running the application and ties up capacity that could be used for other services).

How Does Docker Solve the Responsiveness Problem?

Containers are lightweight wrappers around an application, providing just enough resources for the application to run while ensuring isolation from other containers. Depending on the application, a single server can run many containers, and Docker provides integrated clustering, known as a *swarm*, that allows containers to be deployed without any special awareness of the cluster or configuration changes. The combination of the low resource demands and the integrated clustering means that scaling a containerized ASP.NET Core MVC application is just a matter of adding or removing containers. And, since containers isolate applications, any unused capacity can be repurposed to running containers from another application, allowing workloads to be rebalanced dynamically.

Aren't Docker Containers Just Virtual Machines?

At first glance, containers seem a lot like virtual machines, and there are similarities in the way that containers and virtual machines are used, even if they work in different ways. Both can be used to scale applications by adding or removing instances, and both can be used to create standardized environments for running applications.

But containers are not virtual machines. A virtual machine provides a completely isolated software stack, including the operating system. A single server, for example, can be used to run a mix of virtual machines, each of which can be a different operating system, allowing applications that require Linux and Windows to run side by side in different virtual machines.

Docker only isolates a single application, and all of the containers on a server run on the server's operating system. This means that all the applications run in Linux containers on a Linux server and in Windows containers on a Windows server.

Because Docker containers only isolate applications, they require fewer resources than a virtual machine, which means that a single server can run more containers than it can virtual machines. This doesn't automatically mean that a server running containers can handle more work overall, but it does mean that there are fewer resources spent handling lower-level operating system tasks, which are duplicated in each virtual machine. Figure 1-1 shows the difference between ASP.NET Core MVC applications running in Docker containers and virtual machines.

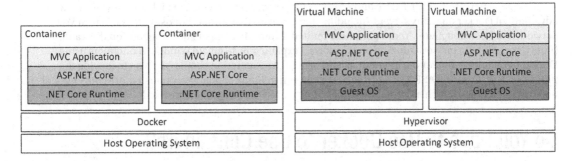

Figure 1-1. *Containers versus virtual machines*

The figure shows the classic comparison between using Docker and virtual machines, but the key difference for ASP.NET Core MVC projects is that Docker provides features that make it easy to create duplicate containers that run alongside one another without any additional configuration, automatically sharing in the application workload by accepting HTTP requests as part of a cluster of containers. This, more than any other difference, is what makes Docker useful because it solves the consistency and responsiveness problems in an elegant way, which is difficult to achieve using traditional virtual machines.

■ **Note**   The comparison in Figure 1-1 shows the difference between containers and virtual machines in a production environment, where containers are run on the host server's operating system. Linux and Windows Server can be used in production. To allow Linux Docker images to be created using macOS and Windows, Docker installs a Linux virtual machine that is used to run containers. The installation and configuration of this virtual machine is done automatically during the installation process in Chapter 3.

Do Docker Containers Have Limitations?

Docker containers are not suited to every project. Containers work best for MVC applications that are stateless, such that a series of HTTP requests from a single client can be handled by more than one instance of the application, running in different containers. This doesn't mean the MVC application cannot have any state data, but it does mean that the state data needs to be stored so it can be accessed from any container, such as by using a database. (I describe how to create an MVC application that accesses a containerized database in Chapter 4.)

Part of the benefit conferred by using Docker is the ability to create and destroy containers as needed, which means that MVC applications that have complex initialization routines, that require manual intervention, or that can run only a single instance are not suitable for containerization.

Docker relies on the containerization support included in server operating systems. The Linux support for containers is mature and reliable and is supported by all of the major distributions. At the time of writing, however, containers are a new addition to Windows Server and are not as mature or as well-supported as their Linux counterparts. Windows containers are available only on Windows Server 2016 and can be developed only using Windows 10 with pre-release versions of Docker. Not all the public cloud platforms provide support for Windows containers, which can restrict your deployment choices.

The good news is that .NET Core and ASP.NET Core work well on Linux, which means you can take advantage of Docker on Linux servers, including those provided by public clouds such as Amazon Web Services and Microsoft Azure. Your options are limited if your MVC application depends on the traditional (non-Core) .NET Framework running on Windows. I explain how to create Windows containers using Docker in Chapter 4, but for the moment at least, careful consideration should be given to moving the project to .NET Core and ASP.NET Core so that it can run in Linux containers, othersiemore conventional deployment methods, such as virtual machines or hosted IIS servers, should be used.

Do You Have to Use Docker to Use Containers?

No. Docker is just one set of tools that work with the container features provided by Linux and Windows. Support for containers has been part of Linux for a long time and has matured into a stable and reliable feature. Microsoft has also embraced containers and has included support for them in Windows Server 2016, although it is not as widely used or as well supported as its Linux counterpart.

Docker has become popular because it makes container functionality easy to use, providing tools that create and manage the images from which containers are created and that cluster those containers together to easily scale applications.

Docker may not suit every need, and since the container support is built into the operating system, there are alternatives to Docker that might be better suited to a specific project. A standardization effort called the Open Container Initiative (https://www.opencontainers.org) aims to standardize the use of containers, which should also make it easier to mix tools and runtimes from other providers. Docker is participating in the standards process, so you should be able to build on the features described in this book even if you use tools or features from other providers.

At the time of writing, the main competitor to Docker is rkt, which is produced by a company called CoreOS and which you can learn about at https://coreos.com/rkt. CoreOS is best known for its lightweight CoreOS Container Linux distribution, which is an excellent server for running containers, including those from Docker. I use CoreOS in Chapter 7 when I demonstrate how to create clusters of servers running containers. CoreOS can also be used on most of the public cloud services that support Docker containers, including Amazon Web Services and Microsoft Azure. See https://coreos.com/why for details of CoreOS Container Linux.

How Do You Set Up Your Development Environment?

Chapter 3 provides detailed setup instructions for Windows, Linux, and macOS.

Contacting the Author

If you have problems making the examples in this book work or if you find a problem in the book, then you can e-mail me at adam@adam-freeman.com and I will try my best to help.

Summary

In this chapter, I described the purpose and content of this book, explained how you can download the project used for each chapter of the book, and explained how Docker solves the consistency and responsiveness problems that face ASP.NET Core MVC applications. In the next chapter, I provide a quick reference to using Docker before showing you how to set up your environment for working with Docker and ASP.NET Core in Chapter 3.

CHAPTER 2

■ ■ ■

Essential Docker Quick Reference

It can be difficult to remember how to perform common tasks when you start working with Docker on your own ASP.NET Core MVC project. This chapter provides a quick reference for the essential Docker features, along with references to the chapters in this book that explain how the features work and demonstrate their use.

Docker Images Quick Reference

Images are the templates from which containers are created. You build on top of a base image to provide a starting point for your projects, obtaining the base image from a repository such as Docker Hub and customizing it using a Docker file. Images and Docker files are described in Chapter 4.

The Docker image used to deploy ASP.NET Core applications does not contain the .NET Core compiler, which means you must use the dotnet publish command to create a directory that contains the compiled code and all of the support files required to run the application. Open a new command prompt and run the following command in your project folder:

```
dotnet publish --framework netcoreapp1.1 --configuration Release --output dist
```

This command publishes the application into a folder called dist, which can be incorporated in the image using the COPY command in a Docker file. The Docker file is processed to create the image using the docker build command.

```
docker build . -t apress/exampleapp -f Dockerfile
```

The first argument is a period, indicating the current working directory, which sets the context directory on which the commands in the Docker file are performed. The -t argument specifies the name of the image, and the -f argument specifies the Docker file. Table 2-1 lists the essential commands for working with images.

© Adam Freeman 2017

A. Freeman, *Essential Docker for ASP.NET Core MVC*, DOI 10.1007/978-1-4842-2778-7_2

Table 2-1. *Essential Commands for Working with Images*

Command	Description
`docker build`	This command processes a Docker file and creates an image.
`docker images`	This command lists the images that are available on the local system. The `-q` argument returns a list of unique IDs that can be used with the `docker rmi` command to remove all images.
`docker pull`	This command downloads an image from a repository.
`docker push`	This command publishes an image to a repository. You may have to authenticate with the repository using the `docker login` command.
`docker tag`	This command is used to associate a name with an image.
`docker rmi`	This command removes images from the local system. The `-f` argument can be used to remove images for which containers exist.

Table 2-2 lists the essential Docker images that are used for ASP.NET Core MVC projects and the examples in this book.

Table 2-2. *The Essential Docker Images for ASP.NET Core MVC Projects*

Image	Description
`microsoft/aspnetcore:1.1.1`	This Linux image contains version 1.1.1 of the .NET Core runtime and the ASP.NET Core packages. This image is used to deploy applications.
`microsoft/dotnet:1.1.1-runtime-nanoserver`	This Windows image contains version 1.1.1 of the .NET Core runtime. This image is used to deploy applications to Windows Server.
`microsoft/aspnetcore-build:1.1.1`	This Linux image contains version 1.1.1 of the .NET Core Software Development Kit. It is used to create development environments in containers.
`mysql:8.0.0`	This Linux image contains version 8 of the MySQL database server.
`haproxy:1.7.0`	This image contains the HAProxy server, which can be used as a load balancer.
`dockercloud/haproxy:1.2.1`	This image contains the HAProxy server, configured to respond automatically to containers starting and stopping.

Images are created using Docker files, which contain a series of commands that describe the container that the image will be used to create. Table 2-3 describes the essential Docker file commands used in this book.

Table 2-3. *The Essential Docker File Commands*

Command	Description
FROM	This command specifies the base image. For ASP.NET Core MVC projects, this command is generally used to select the microsoft/aspnetcore:1.1.1 (for deployment) or microsoft/aspnetcore-build:1.1.1 (for development) images.
WORKDIR	This command changes the working directory for subsequent commands in the Docker file.
COPY	This command adds files so they will become part of the file system of containers that are created from the image.
RUN	This command executes a command as the Docker file is processed. It is commonly used to download additional files to include in the image or to run commands that configure the existing files.
EXPOSE	This command exposes a port so that containers created from the image can receive network requests.
ENV	This command defines environment variables that are used to configure containers created from the image.
VOLUME	This command denotes that a Docker volume should be used to provide the contents of a specific directory.
ENTRYPOINT	This command specifies the application that will be run in containers created from the image.

Docker Containers Quick Reference

Containers are created from an image and used to execute an application in isolation. A single image can be used to create multiple containers that run alongside each other, which is how applications are scaled up to cope with large workloads. You can create containers using custom images or prebuilt images from a public repository such as Docker Hub. Containers are described in Chapter 4 and used throughout the book.

Containers are created using the docker create command, like this:

```
docker create -p 3000:80 --name exampleApp3000 apress/exampleapp
```

Once a container has been created, it can be started using the docker start command.

```
docker start exampleApp3000
```

You can create and start a container in a single step using the docker run command.

```
docker run -p 3000:80 --name exampleApp4000 apress/exampleapp
```

The arguments for these commands are used to configure the container, which allows containers created from the same image to be configured differently. Table 2-4 describes the essential arguments for these commands.

Table 2-4. *Essential Arguments for the docker create and docker run Commands*

Argument	Description
-e, --env	This argument sets an environment variable.
--name	This argument assigns a name to the container.
--network	This argument connects a container to a software-defined network.
-p, --publish	This argument maps a host operating system port to one inside the container.
--rm	This argument tells Docker to remove the container when it stops.
-v, --volume	This argument is used to configure a volume that will provide the contents for a directory in the container's file system.

Table 2-5 lists the essential commands for working with containers.

Table 2-5. *Essential Commands for Working with Containers*

Command	Description
docker create	This command creates a new container.
docker start	This command starts a container.
docker run	This command creates and starts a container in a single step.
docker stop	This command stops a container.
docker rm	This command removes a container.
docker ps	This command lists the containers on the local system. The -a argument includes stopped containers. The -q argument returns a list of unique IDs, which can be used to operate on multiple containers with the docker start, docker stop, and docker rm commands.
docker logs	This command inspects the output generated by a container.
docker exec	This command executes a command in a container or starts an interactive session.

Docker Volumes Quick Reference

Volumes allow data files to be stored outside of a container, which means they are not deleted when the container is deleted or updated. Volumes are described in Chapter 5.

Volumes are defined using the VOLUME command in Docker files, like this:

```
...
VOLUME /var/lib/mysql
...
```

This tells Docker that the files in the /var/lib/mysql folder should be stored in a volume. This is useful only when a named volume is created and applied when configuring the container. Volumes are created using the docker volume create command, like this:

```
docker volume create --name productdata
```

The --name argument is used to specify a name for the volume, which is then used with the -v argument to the docker create or docker run command like this:

```
docker run --name mysql -v productdata:/var/lib/mysql -e MYSQL_ROOT_PASSWORD=mysecret -e
bind-address=0.0.0.0 mysql:8.0.0
```

This command, taken from Chapter 5, tells Docker that the productdata volume will be used to provide the contents of the /var/lib/mysql directory in the container's file system. Removing the container won't remove the volume, which means that any files that are created in the /var/lib/mysql directory won't be deleted, allowing the result of user actions to be stored persistently.

Table 2-6 lists the essential commands for working with volumes.

Table 2-6. *Essential Commands for Working with Volumes*

Command	Description
docker volume create	This command creates a new volume.
docker volume ls	This command lists the volumes that have been created. The -q argument returns a list of unique IDs, which can be used to delete multiple volumes using the docker volume rm command.
docker volume rm	This command removes one or more volumes.

Docker Software-Defined Networks Quick Reference

Software-defined networks are used to connect containers together, using networks that are created and managed using Docker. Software-defined networks are described in Chapter 5.

Software-defined networks are created using the docker network create command, like this:

```
docker network create backend
```

This command creates a software-defined network called backend. Containers can be connected to the network using the --network argument to the docker create or docker start command, like this:

```
docker run -d --name mysql -v productdata:/var/lib/mysql --network=backend -e
MYSQL_ROOT_PASSWORD=mysecret -e bind-address=0.0.0.0 mysql:8.0.0
```

Containers can also be connected to software-defined networks using the docker network connect command, like this:

```
docker network connect frontend productapp1
```

This command connects the container called productapp1 to the software-defined network called frontend.

Table 2-7 lists the essential commands for working with software-defined networks.

Table 2-7. *Essential Commands for Working with Software-Defined Networks*

Command	Description
docker network create	This command creates a new software-defined network.
docker network connect	This command connects a container to a software-defined network.
docker network ls	This command lists the software-defined networks that have been created, including the ones that Docker uses automatically. The -q argument returns a list of unique IDs, which can be used to delete multiple networks using the docker network rm command.
docker network rm	This command removes a software-defined network. There are some built-in networks that Docker creates and that cannot be removed.

Docker Compose Quick Reference

Docker Compose is used to describe complex applications that require multiple containers, volumes, and software-defined networks. The description of the application is written in a compose file, using the YAML format. Docker Compose and compose files are described in Chapter 6, which includes this example compose file:

```
version: "3"

volumes:
  productdata:

networks:
  frontend:
  backend:

services:

  mysql:
    image: "mysql:8.0.0"
    volumes:
      - productdata:/var/lib/mysql
    networks:
      - backend
    environment:
      - MYSQL_ROOT_PASSWORD=mysecret
      - bind-address=0.0.0.0

  dbinit:
    build:
      context: .
      dockerfile: Dockerfile
    networks:
      - backend
```

```
    environment:
      - INITDB=true
      - DBHOST=mysql
    depends_on:
      - mysql

  mvc:
    build:
      context: .
      dockerfile: Dockerfile
    networks:
      - backend
      - frontend
    environment:
      - DBHOST=mysql
    depends_on:
      - mysql
```

This compose file describes an application that contains three services (services are the descriptions from which containers are created), two software-defined networks, and a volume. For quick reference, Table 2-8 describes the configuration keywords from this example compose file.

Table 2-8. *Essential Configuration Keywords Used in Compose Files*

Keyword	Description
version	This keyword specifies the version of the compose file schema. At the time of writing the latest version is version 3.
volume	This keyword is used to list the volumes that are used by the containers defined in the compose file.
networks	This keyword is used to list the volumes that are used by the containers defined in the compose file. The same keyword is used to list the networks that individual containers will be connected to.
services	This keyword is used to denote the section of the compose file that describes containers.
image	This keyword is used to specify the image that should be used to create a container.
build	This keyword is used to denote the section that specifies how the image for a container will be created.
context	This keyword specifies the context directory that will be used when building the image for a container.
dockerfile	This keyword specifies the Docker file that will be used when building the image for a container.
environment	This keyword is used to define an environment variable that will be applied to a container.
depends_on	This keyword is used to specify dependencies between services. Docker doesn't have insight into when applications in containers are ready, so additional steps must be taken to control the startup sequence of an application (as described in Chapter 6).

Docker files are processed using the docker-compose build command like this:

```
docker-compose -f docker-compose.yml build
```

The containers, networks, and volumes in a compose file are created and starting using the docker-compose up command.

```
docker-compose up
```

Table 2-9 lists the essential commands for working with compose files.

Table 2-9. *Essential Commands for Docker Compose*

Command	Description
docker-compose build	This command processes the contents of the compose file and creates the images required for the services it contains.
docker-compose up	This command creates the containers, networks, and volumes defined in the compose file and starts the containers.
docker-compose stop	This command stops the containers created from the services in the compose file. The containers, networks, and volumes are left in place so they can be started again.
docker-compose down	This command stops the containers created from the services in the compose file and removes them, along with the networks and volumes.
docker-compose scale	This command changes the number of containers that are running for a service.
docker-compose ps	This command lists the containers that have been created for the services defined in the compose file.

Docker Swarm Quick Reference

A Docker swarm is a cluster of servers that run containers. There are worker nodes that run the containers and manager nodes that determine which containers run on individual nodes and ensure that the right number of containers are running for each service. Swarms automatically try to recover when containers or nodes fail. Docker swarms are described in Chapter 7.

A swarm is created by running the following command on a manager node:

```
docker swarm init
```

The output from this command includes instructions for setting up the worker nodes, which are configured using the docker swarm join command.

Services can be created manually or described using a compose file. Here is an example of a compose file that includes instructions for deployment into a swarm, taken from Chapter 7:

```
version: "3"

volumes:
  productdata:

networks:
  backend:

services:

  mysql:
    image: "mysql:8.0.0"
    volumes:
      - productdata:/var/lib/mysql
    networks:
      - backend
    environment:
      - MYSQL_ROOT_PASSWORD=mysecret
      - bind-address=0.0.0.0
    deploy:
      replicas: 1
      placement:
        constraints:
        - node.hostname == dbhost

  mvc:
    image: "apress/exampleapp:swarm-1.0"
    networks:
      - backend
    environment:
      - DBHOST=mysql
    ports:
      - 3000:80
    deploy:
      replicas: 5
      placement:
        constraints:
        - node.labels.type == mvc
```

The deploy keyword denotes the configuration section for deploying the services into the swarm. Table 2-10 describes the keywords used in the compose file.

Table 2-10. *The Docker Compose Keywords for Swarms*

Keyword	Description
replicas	This setting specifies how many instances of a container are required for a service.
placement	This configuration section configures the placement of the containers for the service.
constraints	This setting specifies the constraints for locating the containers in the swarm.

Applications that are described using a compose file are deployed using the docker stack deploy command, like this:

```
docker stack deploy --compose-file docker-compose-swarm.yml exampleapp
```

The final argument to this command is used as a prefix applied to the names of the containers, networks, and volumes that are created in the swarm.

Table 2-11 lists the essential commands for working with Docker swarms.

Table 2-11. *Essential Commands for Docker Swarms*

Command	Description
docker swarm init	This command runs on manager nodes to create a swarm.
docker swarm join	This command runs on worker nodes to join a swarm.
docker node ls	This command displays a list of the nodes in the swarm.
docker node update	This command changes the configuration of a node in the swarm.
docker service create	This command manually starts a new service on the swarm.
docker service update	This command changes the configuration of a service running on the swarm.
docker service scale	This command changes the number of containers that are running for a specific service.
docker service ls	This command lists the services that are running on the swarm.
docker service ps	This command lists the containers that are running for a specific service.
docker service rm	This command removes a service from the swarm.
docker stack deploy	This command deploys an application described in a compose file to the swarm.
docker stack rm	This command removes the services described in a compose file from the swarm.

Summary

This chapter provided a quick reference for the Docker features described in the rest of the book. In the next chapter, I show you how to get set up for working with Docker and create the example project that will be used throughout the rest of the book.

CHAPTER 3

■ ■ ■

Getting Ready

In this chapter, I explain how to set up the packages required by ASP.NET Core MVC and Docker and create the example MVC project that is used in the rest of the book. There are instructions for Windows, Linux, and macOS, which are the three operating systems that are supported by both .NET Core and Docker.

Installing the Required Software Packages

The following sections go through the process of installing the packages that are required for ASP.NET Core MVC development and working with Docker. For quick reference, Table 3-1 lists the packages and explains their purpose.

Table 3-1. *The Software Packages Used in This Book*

Name	Description
.NET SDK	The .NET Core Software Development Kit includes the .NET runtime for executing .NET applications and the development tools required to prepare an application for containerization.
Node.js	Node.js is used in this book to run the tools that create the ASP.NET Core MVC project and to download and run Node Package Manager (NPM) packages.
NPM Package	The example application relies on an NPM package to manage its client-side libraries.
Git	Git is a revision control system. It is used indirectly in this book by bower, which is the NPM package that is used to manage client-side packages.
Docker	The Docker package includes the tools and runtime required to create and manage containers. The Windows and macOS versions of Docker include the Docker Compose tool, but it must be installed separately on Linux, as described in Chapter 6.
Visual Studio	Visual Studio is the Windows-only IDE that provides the full-featured development experience for .NET.
Visual Studio Code	Visual Studio Code is a lightweight IDE that can be used on Windows, macOS, and Linux. It doesn't provide the full range of features of the Windows-only Visual Studio product but is well-suited to ASP.NET Core MVC development.

© Adam Freeman 2017

A. Freeman, *Essential Docker for ASP.NET Core MVC*, DOI 10.1007/978-1-4842-2778-7_3

Installing the .NET Core Software Development Kit

The .NET Core Software Development Kit (SDK) includes the runtime and development tools needed to start the development project and to prepare a .NET Core application for use in a container.

Installing the .NET Core SDK on Windows

To install the .NET Core SDK on Windows, download the installer from `https://go.microsoft.com/fwlink/?linkid=843448`. This URL is for the 64-bit .NET Core SDK version 1.1.1, which is the version that I use throughout this book and that you should install to ensure you get the expected results from the examples. (Microsoft also publishes a runtime-only installer, but this does not contain the tools that are required for this book.)

Run the installer, and once the install process is complete, open a new PowerShell command prompt and run the command shown in Listing 3-1 to check that .NET Core is working.

Listing 3-1. Testing .NET Core

```
dotnet --version
```

The output from this command will display the version of the .NET Core runtime that is installed. If you have installed only the version specified earlier, this will be `1.0.1`. (Don't worry that the version number reported by this command doesn't correspond to the version you download; this is expected.)

USING LONG- AND SHORT-FORM COMMAND ARGUMENTS

Most of the examples in this book use the command line, both for .NET and for Docker. There are two types of arguments for commands: long form and short form. The default form, long form, uses two hyphens, like this:

```
dotnet --help
```

This is the long form of the `help` argument. Some commands also have a short-form argument, which uses a single hyphen, like this:

```
dotnet -h
```

Short-form and long-form arguments have the same effect. In this case, they print out a help message. Not all long-form arguments have a short-form equivalent, but you can switch between them freely when they are available.

Installing .NET Core SDK on Linux

The .NET Core SDK can be installed on popular Linux distributions. The easiest way to install .NET Core is to visit `https://www.microsoft.com/net/core`, select your distribution from the list, and copy and paste the commands into a command prompt to ensure you don't mistype any configuration arguments. For completeness, this section shows the installation process for Ubuntu 16.04, which I use throughout this book and which is the current Long Term Support (LTS) release at the time of writing.

To install .NET Core SDK on Ubuntu 16.04, open a command prompt and enter the commands in Listing 3-2 to configure package management so that Microsoft packages can be installed.

Listing 3-2. Preparing Package Management for .NET Core

```
sudo sh -c 'echo "deb [arch=amd64] https://apt-mo.trafficmanager.net/repos/dotnet-
release/ xenial main" > /etc/apt/sources.list.d/dotnetdev.list'
sudo apt-key adv --keyserver hkp://keyserver.ubuntu.com:80 --recv-keys 417A0893
sudo apt-get update
```

Run the command shown in Listing 3-3 to download and install the .NET Core SDK package. It is important that you use the version number shown in the listing so that you get the expected results from the examples in this book.

Listing 3-3. Installing the .NET Core Package

```
sudo apt-get install dotnet-dev-1.0.1
```

Once the package has been downloaded and installed, run the command shown in Listing 3-4 to check that .NET Core is installed and working.

Listing 3-4. Testing the .NET Core Package

```
dotnet --version
```

The output from this command will display the version of the .NET Core runtime that is installed. If you have installed only the version specified earlier, this will be 1.0.1. (Don't worry that the version number reported by this command doesn't correspond to the version you download; this is expected.)

Installing .NET Core on macOS

Before installing .NET Core SDK, open a new command prompt and run the command in Listing 3-5 to install the HomeBrew package manager.

Listing 3-5. Installing the Package Manager

```
/usr/bin/ruby -e \
  "$(curl -fsSL https://raw.githubusercontent.com/Homebrew/install/master/install)"
```

Once installation is complete, run the commands shown in Listing 3-6 to install the OpenSSL library, which is a prerequisite for some .NET Core features.

Listing 3-6. Installing the OpenSSL Package

```
brew install openssl
mkdir -p /usr/local/lib
ln -s /usr/local/opt/openssl/lib/libcrypto.1.0.0.dylib /usr/local/lib/
ln -s /usr/local/opt/openssl/lib/libssl.1.0.0.dylib /usr/local/lib/
```

To install .NET Core on macOS, download the SDK installer from https://go.microsoft.com/ fwlink/?linkid=843444. This URL is for the.NET Core SDK version 1.1.1, which is the version that I use throughout this book and that you should install to ensure you get the expected results from the examples.

Run the installer, and once the process is complete, open a Terminal window and run the command shown in Listing 3-7 at the prompt to check that .NET Core is working.

Listing 3-7. Testing .NET Core

```
dotnet --version
```

The output from this command will display the version of the .NET Core runtime that is installed. If you have installed only the version specified earlier, this will be 1.0.1. (Don't worry that the version number reported by this command doesn't correspond to the version you download; this is expected.)

Installing Node.js

The tools that I use to create the example ASP.NET Core MVC project in this book rely on Node.js (also known as Node), which is a runtime for server-side JavaScript applications and which has become a popular platform for development tools. It is important that you download the same version of Node.js that I use throughout this book. Although Node.js is relatively stable, there are still breaking API changes from time to time that may stop the examples from working.

The version I have used is the 6.9.2 release. You may prefer more recent releases for your own projects, but you should stick with the 6.9.2 release for the rest of this book. A complete set of 6.9.2 releases, with installers for Windows and macOS, is available at https://nodejs.org/dist/v6.9.2. Table 3-2 shows the installer files required for Windows and macOS (Linux installations are handled differently).

Table 3-2. *The Node.js Distribution for Windows and macOS*

Operating System	Node.js Distribution File
Windows 10	https://nodejs.org/dist/v6.9.2/node-v6.9.2-x64.msi
macOS	https://nodejs.org/dist/v6.9.2/node-v6.9.2.pkg

Installing Node.js on Windows

To install Node.js on Windows, download and run the installer listed in Table 3-2. During the installation process, ensure that the npm package manager and Add to PATH options are selected, as shown in Figure 3-1.

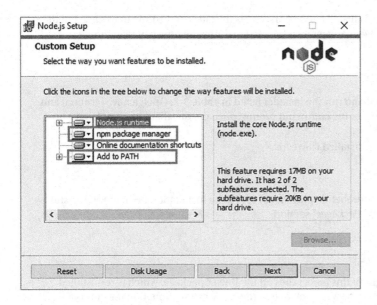

Figure 3-1. *Installing Node.js on Windows*

The NPM package manager is used to download and install Node packages. Adding Node.js to the PATH ensures that you can use the Node.js runtime at the command prompt just by typing node. Once you have completed the installation, open a new command prompt and run the command shown in Listing 3-8.

Listing 3-8. Checking That Node.js Is Installed Correctly

```
node -v
```

You should see the following version number displayed: v6.9.2. If the installation has been successful, then proceed to the "*Installing the NPM Packages*" section.

Installing Node.js on Linux

For Linux, the easiest way to install Node.js is through a package manager, using the procedures described at https://nodejs.org/en/download/package-manager. For Ubuntu, I ran the commands shown in Listing 3-9 to download and install Node.js.

Listing 3-9. Installing Node.js on Ubuntu

```
curl -sL https://deb.nodesource.com/setup_6.x | sudo -E bash -
sudo apt-get install nodejs
```

Once you have installed Node.js, run the command shown in Listing 3-10 to check that the installation has been successful and that you have the right version.

Listing 3-10. Checking That Node.js Is Installed Correctly

```
node -v
```

You should see that version 6.x.x is installed. Version 6.9.2 is the latest at the time of writing, but there may be updates pushed into the package manager feed for version 6.*x* by the time you read this.

Installing Node.js on macOS

To install Node.js on macOS, download and run the installer listed in Table 3-2. Open a new Terminal and run the command shown in Listing 3-11 at the command prompt once the installer has completed.

Listing 3-11. Checking That Node.js Is Installed Correctly

```
node -v
```

You will see the following version number displayed: v6.9.2. If the installation has been successful, then proceed to the "*Installing the NPM Packages*" section.

Installing the NPM Package

The example application used throughout this book relies on the Bower package, which is re-installed using the Node Package Manager (NPM). NPM is included in the Node installation. Run the command shown in Listing 3-12 to install the package that will be used to manage client-side packages in the example application. For macOS and Linux, you need to run this command using sudo or as an administrator.

Listing 3-12. Installing the NPM Packages

```
npm install -g bower@1.8.0
```

There may be a later version of this package available by the time you read this book, but it is important that you use the version specified to ensure that you get the expected results from the examples. Table 3-3 describes the package installed by the command in Listing 3-12.

Table 3-3. *The NPM Package*

Name	Description
bower	Bower is a package manager that handles client-side packages, such as the Bootstrap CSS framework used by the example application in this book.

Installing Git

The Git revision control tool is required to download the client-side packages used by the example ASP.NET Core MVC application created later in this chapter. Visual Studio Code includes integrated Git support, but a separate installation is still required.

Installing Git on Windows or macOS

Download and run the installer from https://git-scm.com/downloads. (On macOS, you may have to change your security settings to open the installer, which has not been signed by the developers.) When the installation is complete, open a new command prompt and run the command in Listing 3-13 to check that Git is installed and working properly.

Listing 3-13. Checking the Git Install

```
git --version
```

This command prints out the version of the Git package that has been installed. At the time of writing, the latest version of Git for Windows is 2.12.0, and the latest version of Git for macOS is 2.10.1.

Installing Git on Linux

Git is already installed on most Linux distributions. If you want to install the latest version, then consult the installation instructions for your distribution at `https://git-scm.com/download/linux`. For Ubuntu, I used the following command:

```
sudo apt-get install git
```

Once you have completed the installation, open a new command prompt and run the command in Listing 3-14 to check that Git is installed and available.

Listing 3-14. Checking the Git Install

```
git --version
```

This command prints out the version of the Git package that has been installed. At the time of writing, the latest version of Git for Linux is 2.7.4.

Installing Docker

Docker supports Windows, macOS, and a range of Linux distributions. The installation process for all platforms is reasonably straightforward, as described in the following sections. Docker is available in Community and Enterprise editions, the difference being the support and certifications offered for the Enterprise edition. Both editions provide the same set of core features, and I use the free Docker Community edition throughout this book.

Installing Docker for Windows

Docker can be used on Windows, taking advantage of the integrated Hyper-V support so that Linux containers can be used.

■ **Note** At the time of writing, only 64-bit versions of Windows 10 Pro, Enterprise, and Education are supported, with the latest updates installed.

Go to https://store.docker.com/editions/community/docker-ce-desktop-windows, click the Get Docker CE for Windows (stable) link, and run the installer that is downloaded. Docker will start automatically when the installation is complete. You may be prompted to enable Hyper-V, as shown in Figure 3-2. Hyper-V allows Linux containers to be used on Windows and must be enabled.

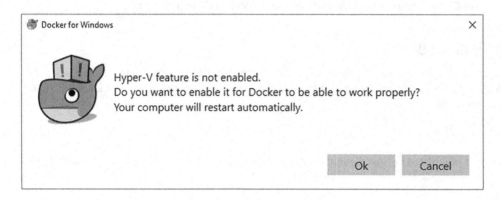

Figure 3-2. Enabling Hyper-V

Once the installation has completed, open a new PowerShell command prompt and run the command shown in Listing 3-15 to check that the installation has been successful.

Listing 3-15. Checking That Docker Is Working

```
docker run --rm hello-world
```

Docker will download the files it needs to run a simple Hello World application. Docker will write out messages like these, indicating that everything is working as expected (the command produces more output than is shown here, but this is the important part):

```
...
Unable to find image 'hello-world:latest' locally
latest: Pulling from library/hello-world

c04b14da8d14: Pull complete
Digest: sha256:0256e8a36e2070f7bf2d0b0763dbabdd67798512411de4cdcf9431a1feb60fd9
Status: Downloaded newer image for hello-world:latest

Hello from Docker!
This message shows that your installation appears to be working correctly.
...
```

INSTALLING DOCKER ON WINDOWS SERVER 2016

If you are creating containers for Windows-only applications, which I demonstrate in Chapter 4, you can run them on Windows Server 2016. This will be of limited appeal for most developers because Linux containers are more widely supported and easier to use, even for ASP.NET Core applications. To install Docker on Windows Server 2016, run the following commands in an Administrative PowerShell:

```
Install-Module -Name DockerMsftProvider -Force
```

```
Install-Package -Name docker -ProviderName DockerMsftProvider -Force
```

These commands install the latest version of Docker. Once the installation has completed, reboot the server and then run the following command to ensure that Docker is installed correctly and working:

```
docker run --rm hello-world:nanoserver
```

Docker will download the files it needs to run a simple Hello World application, which it will run automatically. Docker will write out messages like these, indicating that everything is working as expected (the command produces more output than is shown here, but this is the important part):

```
...
Unable to find image 'hello-world:nanoserver' locally
nanoserver: Pulling from library/hello-world

5496abde368a: Pull complete
482ab31872a2: Pull complete
4256836bcaf8: Pull complete
5bc5abeff404: Pull complete
Digest: sha256:3f5a4d0983b0cf36db8b767a25b0db6e4ae3e5abec8831dc03fe773c58ee404a
Status: Downloaded newer image for hello-world:nanoserver

Hello from Docker!
This message shows that your installation appears to be working correctly.
...
```

Bear in mind that Windows Server 2016 cannot run Linux containers and cannot be used to follow the majority of the examples in this book (or run most of the packages that have been published via Docker).

Installing Docker for Linux

To install Docker on Linux, visit https://www.docker.com/community-edition, select the distribution that you are using from the list, and follow the installation instructions, copying and pasting the commands to avoid typos.

This section shows the installation process for Ubuntu 16.04, which is the distribution I have used throughout this book. Open a new command prompt and enter the commands in Listing 3-16 to configure the package manager and install the prerequisite packages that Docker relies on.

Listing 3-16. Preparing the Package Manager and Installing Prerequisite Packages

```
sudo apt-get -y install apt-transport-https ca-certificates curl
curl -fsSL https://download.docker.com/linux/ubuntu/gpg | sudo apt-key add -
sudo add-apt-repository \
        "deb [arch=amd64] https://download.docker.com/linux/ubuntu \
        $(lsb_release -cs) stable"
sudo apt-get update
```

To install Docker, run the command shown in Listing 3-17.

Listing 3-17. Installing Docker

```
sudo apt-get -y install docker-ce
```

Once Docker is installed, run the commands shown in Listing 3-18 so that you can use Docker without sudo.

Listing 3-18. Configuring Docker So That Root Access Is Not Required

```
sudo groupadd docker
sudo usermod -aG docker $USER
```

Log out of your current session and log back in again for the commands in Listing 3-18 to take effect. Once you have logged back in, run the command shown in Listing 3-19 to check that the installation has been successful.

Listing 3-19. Checking That Docker Is Working

```
docker run --rm hello-world
```

Docker will download the files it needs to run a simple Hello World application. Docker will write out messages like these, indicating that everything is working as expected (the command produces more output than is shown here, but this is the important part):

```
...
Unable to find image 'hello-world:latest' locally
latest: Pulling from library/hello-world

c04b14da8d14: Pull complete
Digest: sha256:0256e8a36e2070f7bf2d0b0763dbabdd67798512411de4cdcf9431a1feb60fd9
Status: Downloaded newer image for hello-world:latest

Hello from Docker!
This message shows that your installation appears to be working correctly.
...
```

Installing Docker on macOS

Go to https://store.docker.com/editions/community/docker-ce-desktop-mac, click the Get Docker for CE Mac (stable) link, and run the installer that is downloaded. Drag the whale to the Applications folder, as shown in Figure 3-3.

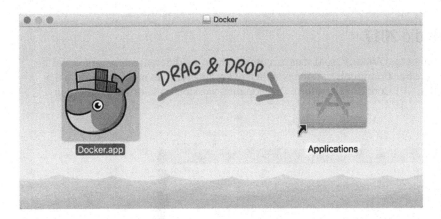

Figure 3-3. Installing Docker

Open Launchpad and click the Docker icon to perform the setup process. At the end of the process, open a new Terminal and run the command shown in Listing 3-20 to check that the installation has been successful.

Listing 3-20. Checking That Docker Is Working

```
docker run --rm hello-world
```

Docker will download the files it needs to run a simple Hello World application. Docker will write out messages like these, indicating that everything is working as expected (the command produces more output than is shown here, but this is the important part):

```
...
Unable to find image 'hello-world:latest' locally
latest: Pulling from library/hello-world

c04b14da8d14: Pull complete
Digest: sha256:0256e8a36e2070f7bf2d0b0763dbabdd67798512411de4cdcf9431a1feb60fd9
Status: Downloaded newer image for hello-world:latest

Hello from Docker!
This message shows that your installation appears to be working correctly.
...
```

Installing an IDE

Although any IDE can be used to develop ASP.NET Core projects, the most common choices are Visual Studio for Windows and Visual Studio Code for macOS and Linux (although you can also use Visual Studio Code on Windows if you wish). Make the choice that suits you best and follow the setup instructions in the sections that follow.

Installing Visual Studio 2017

Download the installer from https://www.visualstudio.com/vs. There are different editions of Visual Studio 2017 available, but the free Community edition is sufficient for the examples in this book. Run the installer and ensure that the .NET Core Cross-Platform Development workload is selected, as shown in Figure 3-4.

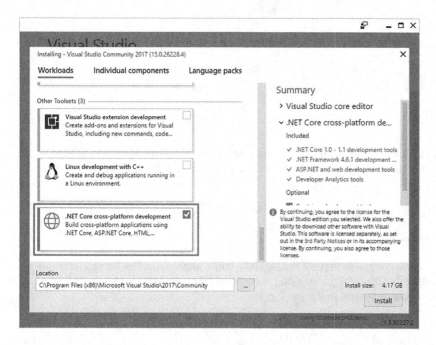

Figure 3-4. *Selecting the Visual Studio packages*

Click the Install button to begin the process of downloading and installing the Visual Studio features.

Adding a YAML Extension to Visual Studio

Some important Docker features are configured using files written in the YAML format. I explain what you need to know to work with these files in Chapter 6, but one aspect of the YAML format that can be frustrating is that tab characters are not allowed. Working with YAML files is made much easier by installing an extension for Visual Studio.

Start Visual Studio and select Extensions and Updates from the Tools menu. Navigate to the Online section, enter **yaml** into the search bar, and click the Download button for the Syntax Highlighting Pack extension, as shown in Figure 3-5. Close Visual Studio and the extension will be installed.

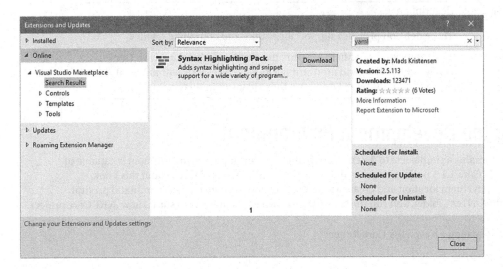

Figure 3-5. *Installing the YAML editing extension*

Installing Visual Studio Code

Visual Studio Code is a lightweight editor that doesn't have all the features of the full Visual Studio product but works across platforms and is perfectly capable of handling ASP.NET Core MVC projects.

Installing Visual Studio Code for Windows and Linux

To install Visual Studio code, visit http://code.visualstudio.com and click the download link for your platform. Run the installer and then start Visual Studio Code, which will present a standard integrated development environment.

Installing Visual Studio Code for macOS

To install Visual Studio code, visit http://code.visualstudio.com and click the Download for Mac link, which will download a zip file. Double-click the downloaded file to decompress it, drag the Visual Studio Code file to the Applications folder, and then use Launch Pad to start Visual Studio Code.

Adding Extensions to Visual Studio Code

There are two packages to install to follow the examples in this book using Visual Studio Code. To install these packages, click the Extensions button in the sidebar and locate and install the packages described in Table 3-4. The Docker Support package is optional, but it can help avoid typos in your Docker configuration files and makes it easier to work with YAML files, which are described in Chapter 6. Restart Visual Studio Code once the extensions are installed.

Table 3-4. *Required Visual Studio Code Packages*

Package Name	Description
C#	This extension provides support for editing and compiling C# files.
Docker	This extension from Microsoft provides support for working with Docker configuration files (and for running Docker commands within Visual Studio Code, although I don't use those features in this book).

Testing the Development Environment

This section contains a simple test to determine whether the development environment is capable of creating a .NET Core 1.1.1 project, which is the version of .NET Core used throughout this book.

Select a convenient location and create a folder called EnvTest. Open a new command prompt, navigate to the EnvTest folder, and run the command shown in Listing 3-21 to start a new .NET Core project.

Listing 3-21. Creating a New .NET Core Project

```
dotnet new console
```

Two files will be created in the EnvTest folder: EnvTest.csproj and Program.cs. If you are using Visual Studio, select Open ➤ Project/Solution from the File menu, navigate to the EnvTest folder, select the EnvTest.csproj file, and click the Open button.

If you are using Visual Studio Code, select Open Folder from the File menu (or Open if you are using macOS), select the EnvTest folder, and click the OK or Select Folder button.

Check the contents of the EnvTest.csproj file to make sure they match Listing 3-22. (If you are using Visual Studio, right-click the EnvTest project item in the Solution Explorer and select Edit EnvTest.csproj from the pop-up menu.)

Listing 3-22. The Contents of the EnvTest.csproj File in the EnvTest Folder

```
<Project Sdk="Microsoft.NET.Sdk">

  <PropertyGroup>
    <OutputType>Exe</OutputType>
    <TargetFramework>netcoreapp1.1</TargetFramework>
  </PropertyGroup>

</Project>
```

Next, open the `Program.cs` file and make the change shown in Listing 3-23.

Listing 3-23. The Contents of the Program.cs File in the EnvTest Folder

```
using System;

namespace ConsoleApplication {
    public class Program {
        public static void Main(string[] args) {
            Console.WriteLine("Essential Docker");
        }
    }
}
```

The code in this file writes out a simple message to the console. Save the changes to the files and run the following command in the EnvTest folder to install the NuGet packages for the project:

```
dotnet restore
```

Next, run the following command in the EnvTest folder to build the code and run the test application:

```
dotnet run
```

This command will compile and run the project. If everything goes well, then you should see output similar to the following, as the code is compiled and the application is run:

```
Essential Docker
```

▪ **Caution**   Do not proceed until you can build and run the test application. The first thing to try is to install the SDK for .NET Core version 1.1.1 using the instructions in the "*Installing .NET Core Software Development Kit*" section of this chapter. If that doesn't work, then try removing all other versions of .NET Core so that only version 1.1.1 is installed. If all else fails and you can't determine the cause of the problem, you can email me at adam@adam-freeman.com and I will try to help you get back on track.

Creating the Example MVC Application

The best way to understand how Docker containers work is to get hands-on experience. This means I need a simple ASP.NET Core MVC project that can be used to demonstrate how you would use Docker containers for your own applications.

▪ **Tip**   You can download the example project from the source repository for this book. See the apress.com page for this book for the URL.

You may be used to relying on the built-in support provided by Visual Studio or Visual Studio Code for creating and managing ASP.NET Core projects, but I rely directly on the command-line tools in this book. As you will learn, working with Docker means understanding how projects work outside of the IDE, which requires familiarity with the .NET command line.

Creating the Project

Select a convenient location and create a folder called ExampleApp. Open a new command prompt, navigate to the ExampleApp folder, and run the command in Listing 3-24 to create a new project with basic ASP.NET Core MVC content.

Listing 3-24. Creating the ASP.NET Core Project

```
dotnet new mvc --language C# --auth None --framework netcoreapp1.1
```

Once the project has been created, run the command shown in Listing 3-25 in the ExampleApp folder to install the NuGet packages it requires.

Listing 3-25. Installing NuGet Packages

```
dotnet restore
```

Opening the Project Using Visual Studio

Select File ➤ Open ➤ Project/Solution from the Visual Studio File menu and navigate to the ExampleApp folder created in the previous section. Select the ExampleApp.csproj file, click the Open button, and Visual Studio will open the project for editing.

Select File ➤ Save All and Visual Studio will prompt you to save a solution file, with the .sln extension. Save this file in the ExampleApp folder and you can use it to open the project in future development sessions.

Opening the Project Using Visual Studio Code

Select Open Folder from the File menu (or Open if you are using macOS), select the ExampleApp folder, and click the OK or Select Folder button. Visual Studio Code will open the folder and display all of the files it contains in the Explorer window. No project or solution files are required when working with Visual Studio Code.

Configuring the Client-Side Packages

Client-side packages in an ASP.NET Core MVC project are conventionally managed using the bower tool, which you installed earlier in this chapter. To specify the client-side packages that will be used, edit the bower.json file in the ExampleApp folder and replace the contents with those shown in Listing 3-26.

Listing 3-26. The Contents of the bower.json File in the ExampleApp Folder

```
{
  "name": "exampleapp",
  "private": true,
  "dependencies": {
    "bootstrap": "4.0.0-alpha.5"
  }
}
```

The only client-side package that I use in the example application is the Bootstrap CSS framework. To download the package, run the following command in the ExampleApp folder:

```
bower install
```

Bower will download the Bootstrap package and store it in the www/lib/bootstrap folder, along with the packages that Bootstrap depends on.

USING THE BOOTSTRAP PRE-RELEASE

Throughout this book, I use a prerelease version of the Bootstrap CSS framework. As I write this, the Bootstrap team is in the process of developing Bootstrap version 4 and has made several early releases. These releases have been labeled as "alpha," but the quality is high, and they are stable enough for use in the examples in this book.

Given the choice of writing this book using the soon-to-be-obsolete Bootstrap 3 and a prerelease version of Bootstrap 4, I decided to use the new version even though some of the class names that are used to style HTML elements are likely to change before the final release. This means you must use the same version of Bootstrap shown in the bowser.json file in Listing 3-30 to get the expected results from the examples.

Creating the Data Model and Repository

I am going to create a simple data model and a repository with some test data. The test data will be a placeholder until Chapter 5, when I introduce a real database that is accessed through Entity Framework Core, the ASP.NET object/relational mapping framework.

Create a folder called ExampleApp/Models and add to it a file called Product.cs, with the content shown in Listing 3-27.

Listing 3-27. The Contents of the Product.cs File in the ExampleApp/Models Folder

```
namespace ExampleApp.Models {

    public class Product {

        public Product() {}

        public Product(string name = null,
                       string category = null,
                       decimal price = 0) {
            Name = name;
            Category = category;
            Price = price;
        }
        public int ProductID { get; set; }
        public string Name { get; set; }
        public string Category { get; set; }
        public decimal Price { get; set; }
    }
}
```

This is the Product model class that I use in the SportsStore application in my *Pro ASP.NET MVC Core* book. It is easy to work with and won't take us too far away from the world of containers.

I like to follow the repository pattern in my MVC applications. I am going to create a dummy repository with static test data to get started and replace it with an implementation that accesses a real database in Chapter 5. To make the transition from static to real data as seamless as possible, I am going to expose the data model through a repository interface, whose implementation will be provided using the ASP.NET Core Dependency Injection feature at runtime.

To define the interface, create a file called IRepository.cs in the ExampleApp/Models folder and add the code shown in Listing 3-28.

Listing 3-28. The Contents of the IRepository.cs File in the ExampleApp/Models Folder

```
using System.Linq;

namespace ExampleApp.Models {

    public interface IRepository {

        IQueryable<Product> Products { get; }
    }
}
```

This interface provides access to a collection of Product objects through a property called Products. A real project would require a repository with support to create and modify objects, but read-only access will be enough functionality for the examples in this book, where the focus is on Docker.

To provide the placeholder test data, add a file called DummyRepository.cs to the ExampleApp/Models folder and add the code shown in Listing 3-29.

Listing 3-29. The Contents of the DummyRepository.cs File in the ExampleApp.Models Folder

```
using System.Linq;

namespace ExampleApp.Models {

    public class DummyRepository : IRepository {
        private static Product[] DummyData = new Product[] {
            new Product { Name = "Prod1",  Category = "Cat1", Price = 100 },
            new Product { Name = "Prod2",  Category = "Cat1", Price = 100 },
            new Product { Name = "Prod3",  Category = "Cat2", Price = 100 },
            new Product { Name = "Prod4",  Category = "Cat2", Price = 100 },
        };

        public IQueryable<Product> Products => DummyData.AsQueryable();

    }
}
```

The DummyRepository class implements the IRepository class, and its Products property returns a collection of Product objects created with static placeholder data. This isn't data you would display to a user, but it is enough to get started with until a real database is added in Chapter 5.

Preparing the Controller and View

An MVC application needs at least one controller and a view to display. Edit the HomeController.cs file in the ExampleApp/Controllers folder and replace the contents with those shown in Listing 3-30.

Listing 3-30. The Contents of the HomeController.cs File in the ExampleApp/Controllers Folder

```
using Microsoft.AspNetCore.Mvc;
using ExampleApp.Models;
using Microsoft.Extensions.Configuration;

namespace ExampleApp.Controllers {
    public class HomeController : Controller {
        private IRepository repository;
        private string message;

        public HomeController(IRepository repo, IConfiguration config) {
            repository = repo;
            message = config["MESSAGE"] ?? "Essential Docker";
        }

        public IActionResult Index() {
            ViewBag.Message = message;
            return View(repository.Products);
        }
    }
}
```

This controller has a constructor that declares a dependency on the IRepository interface, which will be resolved using the ASP.NET dependency injection feature at runtime. There is one action method, called Index, that will be targeted by the default MVC route and that provides its view with the Product objects retrieved from the repository.

The constructor declares a dependency on the IConfiguration interface, which will provide access to the application's configuration. This allows for a configuration setting called MESSAGE to be read, which is passed to the Index action method's view through the view bag and which I use in later chapters to differentiate the results returned by different instances of the MVC application when I show you how to scale up a containerized application.

To provide the view, edit the Index.cshtml file in the ExampleApp/Views/Home folder and replace its contents with those shown in Listing 3-31.

Listing 3-31. The Contents of the Index.cshtml File in the ExampleApp/Views/Home Folder

```
@model IEnumerable<ExampleApp.Models.Product>
@{
    Layout = null;
}
<!DOCTYPE html>
<html>
<head>
    <meta name="viewport" content="width=device-width" />
    <title>ExampleApp</title>
    <link rel="stylesheet" href="~/lib/bootstrap/dist/css/bootstrap.min.css" />
</head>
```

```
<body>
    <div class="m-1 p-1">
        <h4 class="bg-primary text-xs-center p-1 text-white">@ViewBag.Message</h4>
        <table class="table table-sm table-striped">
            <thead>
                <tr><th>ID</th><th>Name</th><th>Category</th><th>Price</th></tr>
            </thead>
            <tbody>
                @foreach (var p in Model) {
                    <tr>
                        <td>@p.ProductID</td>
                        <td>@p.Name</td>
                        <td>@p.Category</td>
                        <td>$@p.Price.ToString("F2")</td>
                    </tr>

                }
            </tbody>
        </table>
    </div>
</body>
</html>
```

The view displays a banner with the message received via the view bag and a table containing the details of the Product objects provided as the view model by the action method.

Configuring ASP.NET and Creating the Entry Point

To configure the application, open the Startup.cs file and replace the contents with the code shown in Listing 3-32, which configures the basic functionality required for an MVC application.

Listing 3-32. The Contents of the Startup.cs File in the ExampleApp Folder

```
using ExampleApp.Models;
using Microsoft.AspNetCore.Builder;
using Microsoft.AspNetCore.Hosting;
using Microsoft.Extensions.DependencyInjection;
using Microsoft.Extensions.Logging;
using Microsoft.Extensions.Configuration;

namespace ExampleApp {
    public class Startup {
        private IConfiguration Configuration;

        public Startup(IHostingEnvironment env) {
            Configuration = new ConfigurationBuilder()
                .SetBasePath(env.ContentRootPath)
                .AddEnvironmentVariables()
                .Build();
        }
```

```
    public void ConfigureServices(IServiceCollection services) {
        services.AddSingleton<IConfiguration>(Configuration);
        services.AddTransient<IRepository, DummyRepository>();
        services.AddMvc();
    }

    public void Configure(IApplicationBuilder app,
            IHostingEnvironment env, ILoggerFactory loggerFactory) {
        loggerFactory.AddConsole();
        app.UseDeveloperExceptionPage();
        app.UseStatusCodePages();
        app.UseStaticFiles();
        app.UseMvcWithDefaultRoute();
    }
}
}
```

Running the MVC Application

If you are using Visual Studio, you can run the project by selecting Start Without Debugging from the Debug menu. A new browser tab or window will open and show the application.

Alternatively, run the following command in the ExampleApp folder to build and run the project from the command line:

```
dotnet run
```

Once the project has started, open a new browser window or tab and navigate to http://localhost:5000, which is the default port used by the built-in server. The browser will show the content illustrated in Figure 3-6, displaying the data from the dummy repository.

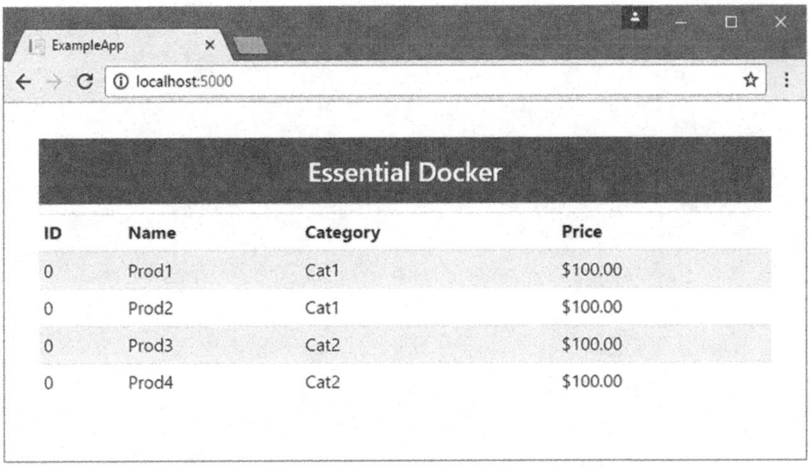

Figure 3-6. Running the example application

Once you have tested the application, type `Control+C` to exit the .NET Core runtime and return control to the command prompt.

Summary

In this chapter, I explained how to install the tools and packages that are required to work on ASP.NET Core MVC packages with Docker and created the example MVC application that will be used in the examples. In the next chapter, I describe the fundamental Docker building blocks: images and containers.

CHAPTER 4

■ ■ ■

Docker Images and Containers

The building blocks for working with Docker are *images* and *containers*. An image is a template for an application and the files required to run it. A container is created from an image and is used to execute the application in isolation so that one application doesn't interfere with another. In this chapter, I explain how to create and use images and containers and demonstrate how to use Docker to containerize an ASP.NET Core MVC application for use on Linux and Windows servers. Table 4-1 puts this chapter in context.

Table 4-1. *Putting Docker Images and Containers in Context*

Question	Answer
What are they?	Images are templates that contain the files that an application needs. Images can be built on top of one another, which makes the process of preparing an image for an application relatively simple.
	Containers are instances of an application created from an image. A single image can be used to create multiple containers, all of which are isolated from one another.
Why are they useful?	Images and containers are the key Docker building blocks. Images can be published to the Docker Hub so they can be used more widely, either within your organization or publicly.
How are they used?	Images are created using instructions contained in a Docker file using the docker build command. Containers are created from an image using docker create and are started and stopped using docker start and docker stop.
Are there any pitfalls or limitations?	For complex applications, the process of writing a Docker file, using it to create an image, and then testing a container generated from that image can be a time-consuming process.
Are there any alternatives?	No. Images and containers are core Docker features.

© Adam Freeman 2017
A. Freeman, *Essential Docker for ASP.NET Core MVC*, DOI 10.1007/978-1-4842-2778-7_4

Table 4-2 summarizes the chapter.

Table 4-2. *Chapter Summary*

Problem	Solution	Listing
List the images that are available on the local system	Use the docker images command	1
Download an image from a repository	Use the docker pull command	2, 3
Delete images	Use the docker rmi command	4, 5, 29
Create a custom image	Create a Docker file and use it with the docker build command	6, 8, 34
Prepare an ASP.NET Core MVC application for containerization	Use the dotnet publish command	7, 35
Create a container	Use the docker create command	9, 10
List the containers on the local system	Use the docker ps command	11
Start a container	Use the docker start command	12, 13, 20
Stop a container	Use the docker stop command	14, 15, 19
See the output from a container	Use the docker logs command	16, 17
Create and start a container in a single step	Use the docker run command	18, 36
Copy a file into a container	Use the docker cp command	21, 22
See the changes in a container's file system	Use the docker diff command	23
Run a command in a container	Use the docker exec command	24–26, 38–40
Create an image from a modified container	Use the docker commit command	27
Assign a tag to an image	Use the docker tag command	28, 32
Manage authentication with a repository	Use the docker login and docker logout commands	30, 33
Publish an image to a repository	Use the docker push command	31, 32
View the configuration of a container	Use the docker inspect command	37

Preparing for This Chapter

This chapter depends on the ExampleApp MVC project and the tools and packages from Chapter 3. If you don't want to work through the process of creating the example application, you can get the project as part of the free source code download that accompanies this book. See the apress.com page for this book.

Working with Images

Images are templates that are used to create containers and that contain a file system with all the files the application in the container requires. When you tested Docker in Chapter 3, the command you used instructed Docker to use an image called hello-world, which has been published to the public repository of images, known as the Docker Hub.

The hello-world image contains all the files required by an application that prints out a simple greeting, providing a self-contained way to distribute the files so they can be used to run the application. Run the command shown in Listing 4-1 to list the images installed on your system.

Listing 4-1. Listing the Available Images

```
docker images
```

The response to the command is a list of the images that are available locally, like this:

```
REPOSITORY       TAG       IMAGE ID        CREATED         SIZE
hello-world      latest    c54a2cc56cbb    4 months ago    1.848 kB
```

There is only one image shown in this output, which is the hello-world image. When Docker downloads images to create containers, it stores them locally to speed up future tasks.

Downloading Images

The docker pull command is used to download an image from the repository so that it is available locally. This isn't something you usually need to do explicitly because other Docker commands that manage images and containers will automatically pull the images they need. Run the command shown in Listing 4-2 to pull an image from the Docker Hub.

Listing 4-2. Pulling an Image from the Docker Hub

```
docker pull alpine
```

It can take a while for Docker to download the image, which contains an embedded version of Linux called Alpine. This image doesn't have any bearing on .NET development, but it is relatively small, which means that it can be downloaded quickly.

When the new image has been downloaded, run the docker images command and you will see that the list has been updated.

```
REPOSITORY       TAG       IMAGE ID        CREATED         SIZE
alpine           latest    baa5d63471ea    8 weeks ago     4.803 MB
hello-world      latest    c54a2cc56cbb    5 months ago    1.848 kB
```

Repository images can be tagged, allowing different versions of an image to coexist and ensuring that you get the right version of an image when you pull it. A tag is specified by appending a colon (the : character) to the image name, followed by the tag. Run the command in Listing 4-3 to pull a variation of the alpine image.

Listing 4-3. Pulling an Image Variation

```
docker pull alpine:3.4
```

This command pulls the version of the `alpine` image that has been tagged as `3.4`, indicating that the image contains version 3.4. When the image has been downloaded, the `docker images` command will show the variations in the list.

```
REPOSITORY      TAG        IMAGE ID        CREATED         SIZE
alpine          3.4        baa5d63471ea    8 weeks ago     4.803 MB
alpine          latest     baa5d63471ea    8 weeks ago     4.803 MB
hello-world     latest     c54a2cc56cbb    5 months ago    1.848 kB
```

The images have the same `IMAGE ID` because they contain identical content, meaning that the `alpine` maintainers have tagged the same image with two different tags. Docker is smart enough to know that it has the content that it requires already and won't download a duplicate image. (You may not see the same IDs if a more recent version of Alpine has been released by the time you read this chapter.)

Omitting the image tag is equivalent to requesting the variation tagged `latest`, so `docker pull alpine` and `docker pull alpine:latest` are equivalent commands. Since I didn't specify a tag when I pulled the earlier `alpine` image or the `hello-world` image used in Chapter 3, the `latest` versions were retrieved.

■ **Tip**   You can see which tags are available for an image by going to the Docker Hub (`https://hub.docker.com`) and searching for an image.

Deleting Images

The `docker rmi` command is used to remove one or more images from your machine. Images are deleted by specifying their unique ID.

Run the command shown in Listing 4-4 to delete the `alpine:3.4` image, using the ID shown by `docker images`. (You might not have the same ID, which may have changed since I wrote this chapter. Check the output from the `docker images` command to see which ID you need to use for this command.)

Listing 4-4. Deleting an Image by ID

```
docker rmi -f baa5d63471ea
```

Run the `docker images` command again and you will see that both `alpine` images have been removed, since both images had the specified ID. The `-f` argument is used to remove images even when they are being used by containers (which I describe later in the chapter).

Copying and pasting individual image IDs is a tedious and error-prone process. If you want to delete all the images you have installed, then you can use the command in Listing 4-5.

Listing 4-5. Deleting All Images

```
docker rmi -f $(docker images -q)
```

The `-q` argument specifies the oddly named quiet mode, which returns only the `IMAGE ID` values from the `docker images` command, which are processed by the `docker rmi` command, removing all the images in the list.

Creating a Docker File for a Custom Image

The Docker Hub contains a wide range of images for prepackaged applications, but for ASP.NET Core development, the real power of Docker comes from being able to create custom images for MVC applications.

Custom images are described in a Docker file, conventionally named Dockerfile, which contains a series of instructions that Docker follows like a recipe.

To demonstrate how custom images work, I am going to create one for the example application from Chapter 3. Open the Dockerfile that was added to the project and replace the contents with those shown in Listing 4-6.

Listing 4-6. The Contents of the Dockerfile File in the ExampleApp Folder

```
FROM microsoft/aspnetcore:1.1.1

COPY dist /app

WORKDIR /app

EXPOSE 80/tcp

ENTRYPOINT ["dotnet", "ExampleApp.dll"]
```

These five commands are all that's required to create a Docker image for the example application. Each of the commands is described in detail in the sections that follow.

Setting the Base Image

One of the most powerful features of Docker images is that they can be based on existing images, meaning that they include all the files that the base image contains. The FROM command is the first command in a Docker file, and it specifies the base image that will be used.

In this case, the base image is called microsoft/aspnetcore, and I have specified that the version tagged 1.1.1 should be used, which contains .NET Core and ASP.NET Core version 1.1.1.

```
...
FROM microsoft/aspnetcore:1.1.1
...
```

This image is produced by Microsoft, and it contains the .NET Core runtime and the ASP.NET Core packages, compiled into native code to improve application startup. This image doesn't contain the .NET SDK, which means the MVC application must be prepared before it is used in the image, as demonstrated in the *"Preparing the Application for the Image"* section.

■ **Tip**   I show you how to create a containerized development environment in Chapter 8, which uses a base image that does include the .NET SDK.

Copying the Application Files

When you containerize an ASP.NET Core application, all the compiled class files, NuGet packages, configuration files, and the Razor views are added to the image. The COPY command copies files or folders into the container.

```
...
COPY dist /app
...
```

This command copies the files from a folder called dist into a folder called /app in the container. The dist folder doesn't exist at the moment, but I'll create it when I prepare the MVC project for use with the container.

Setting the Working Directory

The WORKDIR command sets the working directory for the container, which is useful if you need to run commands or use files without having to specify the full path each time. The command in the Docker file sets the path to the /app folder that the COPY command created and that contains the application files.

Exposing the HTTP Port

Processes inside a container can open network ports without any special measures, but Docker won't allow the outside world to access them unless the Docker file contains an EXPOSE command that specifies the port number, like this:

```
...
EXPOSE 80/tcp
...
```

This command tells Docker that it can make port 80 available for TCP traffic from outside the container. For the example application, this is required so that the ASP.NET Core Kestrel server can receive HTTP requests.

■ **Tip**   Working with ports in containers is a two-step process. See the "*Working with Containers*" section for details of how to complete the configuration so that the server can receive requests.

Running the Application

The final step in the Docker file is the ENTRYPOINT command, which tells Docker what to do when the container starts.

```
...
ENTRYPOINT ["dotnet", "ExampleApp.dll"]
...
```

This command tells Docker to run the `dotnet` command-line tool to execute the `ExampleApp.dll` file, which I will create in the next section. The path to the `ExampleApp.dll` file doesn't have to be specified because it is assumed to be within the directory specified by the `WORKDIR` command, which will contain all the application's files.

Preparing the Application for the Image

There are some entries in the Docker file that may not make immediate sense, especially if you are used to working with ASP.NET Core MVC projects through Visual Studio or Visual Studio Code.

The base image specified by the Docker file in Listing 4-6 doesn't include the .NET Core SDK, which means that the compiler isn't available and the MVC project files cannot be compiled automatically when the application is started, which is what usually happens in development.

Instead, the application has to be compiled before it is incorporated into the image. Run the commands in Listing 4-7 from the `ExampleApp` folder to prepare the example application.

Listing 4-7. Preparing the Example Application in the ExampleApp Folder

```
dotnet restore
dotnet publish --framework netcoreapp1.1 --configuration Release --output dist
```

The `dotnet restore` command is a precautionary step to make sure that the project has all the NuGet packages it needs.

The important command is `dotnet publish`, which compiles the application and then transforms it into a stand-alone set of files that includes everything the application requires. The `--output` argument specifies that the compiled project should be written to a folder called `dist`, which corresponds to the `COPY` command from the Docker file. The `--framework` argument specifies that .NET Core version 1.1.1 should be used, and the `--configuration` argument specifies that the `Release` mode should be used.

Look at the contents of the `dist` folder when the `dotnet publish` command has completed and you will see that one of the files is called `ExampleApp.dll`. This file contains the custom code from the example project and provides the entry point for running the application, corresponding to the `ENTRYPOINT` command in the Docker file.

Creating a Custom Image

To process the Docker file and generate the image for the example application, run the command shown in Listing 4-8 in the `ExampleApp` folder.

Listing 4-8. Creating a Custom Image in the ExampleApp Folder

```
docker build . -t apress/exampleapp -f Dockerfile
```

The `docker build` command creates a new image. The period that follows the `build` keyword provides the *context*, which is the location that is used for commands such as `COPY` in the Docker file. The `-t` argument tags the new image as `apress/exampleapp`, and the `-f` argument specifies the Docker file that contains the instructions for creating the image. (The convention for naming images is to use your name or your organization's name, followed by the application name.)

Docker will download the base images it needs and then follow the instructions in the Docker file to generate the new image. When the build process has completed, you can see the new image by running the docker images command, which will produce output like this:

```
REPOSITORY            TAG       IMAGE ID        CREATED         SIZE
apress/exampleapp     latest    e2e0945a741d    4 seconds ago   280 MB
microsoft/aspnetcore  1.1.1     da08e329253c    23 hours ago    268 MB
```

The apress/exampleapp image is the custom image containing the MVC application. The microsoft/aspnetcore image is shown because Docker had to pull that image from the Docker Hub when it followed the FROM command in the Docker file.

Working with Containers

Containers bring images to life. Each container is an instance of an application created from an image, and a host system can run multiple containers, each of which is isolated from the others. In the sections that follow, I explain how to create, use, and manage containers.

Creating Containers

Containers can be created from any image, including custom images you have created.

Run the command shown in Listing 4-9 to create a new container using the custom image from the previous section as the template.

Listing 4-9. Creating a Container

```
docker create -p 3000:80 --name exampleApp3000 apress/exampleapp
```

The docker create command is used to create a new image.

The -p argument to the docker create command tells Docker how to map port 80 inside the container to the host operating system. In this case, I have specified that port 80 inside the container should be mapped to port 3000 in the host operating system. This corresponds to the EXPOSE command in the Docker file in Listing 4-6.

The --name argument assigns a name to the container, which makes it easier to work with once it has been created. The name in this case is exampleApp3000, indicating that this container will respond to requests sent to port 3000 in the host operating system.

The final argument tells Docker which image to use as the template for the new container. This command specifies the apress/exampleapp image, which is the name used with the docker build command in Listing 4-8.

Creating Additional Containers from an Image

You can create more than one container from an image, but you must ensure that there are no conflicts for configuration options such as names and port mappings. Run the command shown in Listing 4-10 to create a second container using the custom image with a different name and port mapping.

Listing 4-10. Creating Another Container

```
docker create -p 4000:80 --name exampleApp4000 apress/exampleapp
```

This command creates a container called exampleApp4000 using the apress/exampleapp image but maps port 80 to port 4000 in the host. This container will be able to coexist with the exampleApp3000 container because they use different network ports and names, even though they contain the same application.

Listing Containers

The docker ps command is used to list the containers that exist on a system. By default, the docker ps command omits containers that are not running, so the -a argument must be used if you want to see all the containers that are available, as shown in Listing 4-11.

Listing 4-11. Listing All Containers

```
docker ps -a
```

This command produces the following output, showing the two containers created in the previous section (I have shown only the most important columns to fit the output on the page):

```
CONTAINER ID    IMAGE              STATUS     PORTS     NAMES
765b418bc16f    apress/exampleapp  Created              exampleApp4000
136b2a3e2246    apress/exampleapp  Created              exampleApp3000
```

Each container is assigned a unique ID, which is shown in the CONTAINER ID column and can be used to refer to the container in Docker commands. A more natural way to refer to containers is using their name, which is shown in the NAMES column. The IMAGE column shows the image used to create the container.

The STATUS column shows Created for both containers, indicating that the containers have been successfully created and are ready to be started. The PORTS column is empty because neither of the containers has any active network ports at the moment, but that will change when the containers are active.

Starting Containers

The previous section used the docker create command to create two containers from the same image. These containers are identical on the inside and contain identical files. Only the configuration outside the containers is different, allowing the containers to coexist by using different names and mapping different network ports to port 80 inside the container.

At the moment, however, the containers are not doing anything. The applications they contain are not running, and the network ports they have been configured to use are not active.

The docker start command is used to start one or more containers, which are referred to by their unique ID or by their name. Run the command shown in Listing 4-12 to start the container that is called exampleApp3000.

Listing 4-12. Starting a Container

```
docker start exampleApp3000
```

Docker will use the ENTRYPOINT command from the Docker file to start the application in the container. In this case, that means the .NET Core runtime is started, followed by the ASP.NET Core Kestrel server, which will listen for incoming HTTP requests on port 80 inside the container.

As the container is started, Docker will also set up the port mapping so that network traffic received on port 3000 on the host operating system will be directed to port 80 inside the container, allowing Kestrel to receive HTTP requests from outside the container.

To test the container, open a new browser window and request the URL http://localhost:3000, which will send an HTTP request to port 3000 on the host operating system. Docker will direct the request to port 80 inside the container, which allows it to be received by Kestrel, which will start ASP.NET Core MVC and run the example application.

After a couple of seconds, you will see the response from the example MVC application, as shown in Figure 4-1. Reload the browser window to send another request to the same URL and you will see that it is much faster now that the application is up and running.

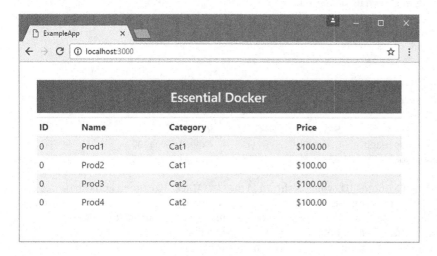

Figure 4-1. *Running the example application*

Run the command shown in Listing 4-13 to start all the containers on a system.

Listing 4-13. Starting All Containers

```
docker start $(docker ps -aq)
```

The command combines docker start with the output of the docker ps command. The -a argument includes containers that are not running, and the -q argument returns just the container IDs.

Since one of the containers is already running, the command has the effect of starting the container that is mapped to port 4000, which you can test by requesting the URL http://localhost:4000 in the browser window, which will show the same content as Figure 4-1 because both containers are running the same application.

You can see the container's change in status by running the docker ps -a command, which will produce output like this:

```
CONTAINER ID  IMAGE              STATUS         PORTS                 NAMES
765b418bc16f  apress/exampleapp  Up 4 seconds   0.0.0.0:4000->80/tcp  exampleApp4000
136b2a3e2246  apress/exampleapp  Up 9 minutes   0.0.0.0:3000->80/tcp  exampleApp3000
```

The STATUS column reports that both containers are Up and how long they have been running for. The PORTS column shows the ports that each container has mapped from the host operating system. In this case, you can see that one container maps port 3000 to port 80 and the other maps port 4000 also to port 80.

These containers can coexist because the applications within the containers are isolated from each other and have no knowledge of the port mapping system. The Kestrel server that is handling HTTP requests inside the container starts listening to port 80, unware that it is running in a container and unware that the requests are coming through a port mapping on the host operating system. The ability to create multiple containers from the same image and run them side by side by varying their configuration is a key feature of Docker and is illustrated by Figure 4-2. I return to this topic in Chapter 6, when I demonstrate how to scale up an application, and in Chapter 7, when I show you how to deploy and application into a server cluster.

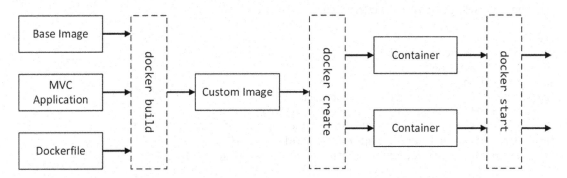

Figure 4-2. *The path from image to container to service*

Stopping Containers

Containers are stopped using the docker stop command, which can stop one or more containers by name or by ID. Run the command in Listing 4-14 to stop the container that is handling requests on port 3000.

Listing 4-14. Stopping a Container Using Its Name

```
docker stop exampleApp3000
```

Run the command shown in Listing 4-15 to stop all the running containers, using the list of containers generated by the docker ps command.

Listing 4-15. Stopping All Containers

```
docker stop $(docker ps -q)
```

The only argument required for the docker ps command is -q. The -a argument is not used because only the IDs of running containers are needed for the stop command, and this is what the ps command returns by default.

■ **Tip** There is also a docker kill command, which sends a SIGKILL signal to the container. I tend not to use this command since docker stop will automatically send this signal if the container hasn't stopped after ten seconds, a period that can be changed using the -t argument.

Getting Container Output

By default, Docker doesn't display the output from the application when you start a container using the docker start command. But it does keep a record that can be inspected using the docker logs command, as shown in Listing 4-16.

Listing 4-16. Getting Container Logs

```
docker logs exampleApp3000
```

The ASP.NET Core runtime writes out a message each time it receives an HTTP request, and the docker logs command displays those messages, which look like this:

```
...
Hosting environment: Production
Content root path: /app
Now listening on: http://+:80
Application started. Press Ctrl+C to shut down.
info: Microsoft.AspNetCore.Hosting.Internal.WebHost[1]
      Request starting HTTP/1.1 GET http://localhost:3000/
info: Microsoft.AspNetCore.Mvc.Internal.ControllerActionInvoker[1]
      Executing action method ExampleApp.Controllers.HomeController.Index
        (ExampleApp) with arguments ((null)) - ModelState is Valid
...
```

The docker logs command shows you the most recent output from the container, even after the container has been stopped. For running containers, you can use the -f argument to monitor the output so that you will see any new messages that are produced. Run the commands in Listing 4-17 to start a container and monitor its output.

Listing 4-17. Following a Container's Logs

```
docker start exampleApp3000
docker logs -f exampleApp3000
```

Request http://localhost:3000 in the browser to generate some output messages. When you are done, type Control+C to stop the displaying the output. The container is unaffected by the docker logs command and continues running in the background.

Creating and Starting Containers with a Single Command

The docker run command is used to create a container from an image and start it in a single step, combining the effects of the docker create and docker start commands. Run the command in Listing 4-18 to create and start a container from the custom image, with a port mapping that forwards network traffic from port 5000 in the host operating system to port 80 inside the container.

Listing 4-18. Creating and Running a Container with a Single Command

```
docker run -p 5000:80 --name exampleApp5000 apress/exampleapp
```

This command takes the same arguments as the docker create command from Listing 4-10: it tells Docker to create the container from the apress/exampleapp image, sets up the port mapping, and assigns the container the name exampleApp5000.

The difference is that the container is started once it has been created. The docker run command keeps the command prompt attached to the container output so that the messages generated by the Kestrel server are displayed in the command prompt.

To test the new container, open a browser tab and request the URL http://localhost:5000. The HTTP request that it sends to port 5000 will be received by Docker and forwarded to port 80 inside the container, producing the same response from the MVC application you saw in earlier examples.

If you are using Linux or macOS, you can stop the container by typing Control+C. If you are using Windows, Control+C detaches the command prompt from the container but leaves it running in the background, and you will have to run the command in Listing 4-19 to stop the container.

Listing 4-19. Stopping a Container

```
docker stop exampleApp5000
```

REMOVING CONTAINERS AUTOMATICALLY

The docker run command can be used with the --rm argument, which tells Docker to remove the container when it stops. Run this command to create a container that maps port 6500 in the host container to port 80 in the new container:

```
docker run -p 6500:80 --rm --name exampleApp6500 apress/exampleapp
```

You can test the container by requesting http://localhost:6500 in the browser and by running docker ps. Once you have checked that the container is working, stop the container using Control+C (for Linux or macOS) or using this command (Windows).

```
docker stop exampleApp6500
```

Docker will remove the container as soon as it stops, which you can confirm by running docker ps -a to see all the containers that exist on the system.

Modifying Containers

Images are immutable, but containers are not. Each container has its own writable file system. If you create two containers from the same image, they will be identical at first and contain the same files. But, as the applications in the containers run, the data and log files they create can cause the containers to become different, with content that reflects the user requests they process.

You can also modify a container deliberately, using the Docker tools, and then use those changes to create a new image that, in turn, can be used to create containers. This can be useful if you need to perform some kind of manual configuration to allow an application to work properly in a container. In the sections that follow, I show you different ways to make changes and then use those changes to generate a new image.

Changing a Container

To understand how containers can be changed, run the command in Listing 4-20 to ensure that the MVC containers with mappings to ports 3000 and 4000 are running.

Listing 4-20. Starting the MVC Application Containers

```
docker start exampleApp3000 exampleApp4000
```

These containers were created from the same image and contain an identical Razor view, which is used to generate a response for the MVC application's default URL. Confirm that the applications in both containers generate the same response by opening browser tabs and requesting the URLs `http://localhost:3000` and `http://localhost:4000`, as shown in Figure 4-3.

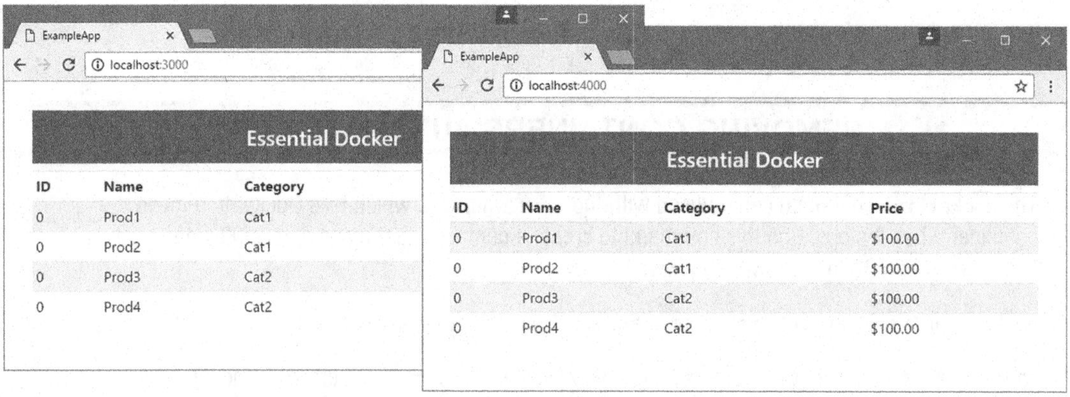

Figure 4-3. *Responses from the containerized MVC applications*

Each container has its own writeable file system, which can be modified independently of the other containers created from the same image. To create a change that has a visible effect, use your IDE to change the message displayed in the banner in the Razor view in the `ExampleApp/Views/Home` folder, as shown in Listing 4-21.

Listing 4-21. Modifying the View in the Index.cshtml File in the ExampleApp/Views/Home Folder

```
@model IEnumerable<ExampleApp.Models.Product>
@{
    Layout = null;
}
<!DOCTYPE html>
<html>
<head>
    <meta name="viewport" content="width=device-width" />
    <title>ExampleApp</title>
    <link rel="stylesheet" href="~/lib/bootstrap/dist/css/bootstrap.min.css" />
</head>
```

```
<body>
    <div class="m-1 p-1">
        <h4 class="bg-success text-xs-center p-1 text-white">This is new content</h4>
        <table class="table table-sm table-striped">
            <thead>
                <tr><th>ID</th><th>Name</th><th>Category</th><th>Price</th></tr>
            </thead>
            <tbody>
                @foreach (var p in Model) {
                    <tr>
                        <td>@p.ProductID</td>
                        <td>@p.Name</td>
                        <td>@p.Category</td>
                        <td>$@p.Price.ToString("F2")</td>
                    </tr>
                }
            </tbody>
        </table>
    </div>
</body>
</html>
```

The changes apply a different Bootstrap background class and change the content in the h4 element. At the moment, the changed Razor view exists in the ExampleApp folder of the host operating system and has no effect on the containers.

Run the command shown in Listing 4-22 from the ExampleApp folder to copy the view into one of the containers.

Listing 4-22. Modifying a Container

```
docker cp ./Views/Home/Index.cshtml exampleApp3000:/app/Views/Home/
```

The docker cp command is used to copy files in and out of containers. This command copies the modified Index.cshtml file from the project folder in the host operating system into the /app/Views folder in the exampleApp3000 folder, which is the folder from which the MVC application inside the container gets its views.

To see the effect of the change, use your browser to request the URL http://localhost:3000. The MVC application in the container that receives the HTTP request will detect the changed file, compile it into a C# class, and use it to generate a response, as shown in Figure 4-4.

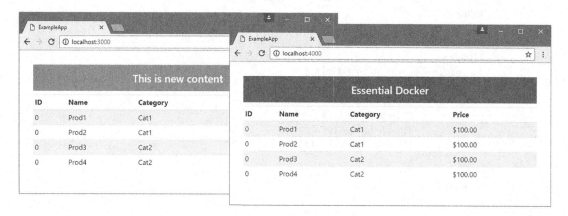

Figure 4-4. *Modifying a file in a container*

The figure also shows the response you will see when you request the URL http://localhost:4000. This illustrates that each container has its own storage and that changes to one container do not affect the other. The changes to a container's file system are persistent, which means you can stop and start the modified container and the change made by the command in Listing 4-22 will still be used.

■ **Caution**   Modifying files in containers should be done with caution and never done to a container in production. See Chapter 8 if you want to change the files in an application because you are actively developing the project, where I explain how to create a containerized development environment.

Examining Changes to a Container

Run the command shown in Listing 4-23 to see the changes to the container's file system.

Listing 4-23. Examining Container Changes

```
docker diff exampleApp3000
```

The docker diff command shows the differences between the files in the container and the image that was used to create it and produces output like this (you may see slightly different results):

```
C /app
C /app/Views
C /app/Views/Home
C /app/Views/Home/Index.cshtml
C /root
A /root/.aspnet
A /root/.aspnet/DataProtection-Keys
```

```
C /tmp
A /tmp/clr-debug-pipe-1-1154405-in
A /tmp/clr-debug-pipe-1-1154405-out
```

Each entry in the results is annotated with a letter that indicates the type of change, as described in Table 4-3.

Table 4-3. *The Change Annotations from the docker diff Command*

Annotation	Description
A	This annotation indicates that a file or folder has been added to the container
C	This annotation indicates that a file or folder has been modified. For folders, a change indicates that a file has been added or removed inside that folder.
D	This annotation indicates that a file or folder has been removed from the container.

In addition to the change I made to the Index.cshtml file, you can see that some files have been created by the ASP.NET Core runtime. Some of files are related to debugging, which I show you how to perform in a container in Chapter 8.

Executing Commands in Containers

An alternative to copying files in and out of containers is to interact with the container directly, executing commands inside the container. This is a technique that should be used with caution, but it can be useful to run configuration tasks or to diagnose problems with a container once it is running.

Run the command in Listing 4-24 to list the content of the Razor view file in one of the containers.

Listing 4-24. Executing a Command

```
docker exec exampleApp3000 cat /app/Views/Home/Index.cshtml
```

The docker exec command is used to execute commands inside the container. The name of the container is followed by the command and any arguments that it requires. You can use only the commands that are available within the container. The command in Listing 4-24 tells the container to use the Linux cat command to list the contents of the Razor view file, which will produce the following response:

```
@model IEnumerable<ExampleApp.Models.Product>
@{
    Layout = null;
}
<!DOCTYPE html>
<html>
<head>
    <meta name="viewport" content="width=device-width" />
    <title>ExampleApp</title>
    <link rel="stylesheet" href="~/lib/bootstrap/dist/css/bootstrap.min.css" />
</head>
```

```
<body>
    <div class="m-1 p-1">
        <h4 class="bg-success text-xs-center p-1 text-white">This is new content</h4>
        <table class="table table-sm table-striped">
            <thead>
                <tr><th>ID</th><th>Name</th><th>Category</th><th>Price</th></tr>
            </thead>
            <tbody>
                @foreach (var p in Model) {
                    <tr>
                        <td>@p.ProductID</td>
                        <td>@p.Name</td>
                        <td>@p.Category</td>
                        <td>$@p.Price.ToString("F2")</td>
                    </tr>

                }
            </tbody>
        </table>
    </div>
</body>
</html>
```

■ **Tip**   Use the `docker start` command to make sure that a container is running before you use `docker exec`.

An extension of the ability to execute commands is to run an interactive shell, which can be more convenient if the work you need to do on a container involves chaining together several steps or would be easier with features such as file completion for navigating around the file system.

The base Linux image that is used for ASP.NET Core containers includes the Bash shell, which you can start by running the command shown in Listing 4-25.

Listing 4-25. Starting a Shell in a Container

```
docker exec -it exampleApp3000 /bin/bash
```

The `-it` argument to the `docker exec` command tells Docker that this is an interactive command that requires terminal support. Once the interactive shell has started, run the commands in Listing 4-26 to modify the contents of the Razor view in the MVC application.

Listing 4-26. Modifying the Razor View in the Bash Shell

```
cd /app/Views/Home
sed -i "s/new content/interactive content/g" Index.cshtml
exit
```

The first command changes the working directory to the folder that contains the view. The second command uses `sed` to replace the phrase new content with interactive content inside the view file. The final command, exit, quits the shell and leaves the container to run in the background.

You can see the effect of the change by using the browser to navigate to `http://localhost:3000`, which will produce the result shown in Figure 4-5.

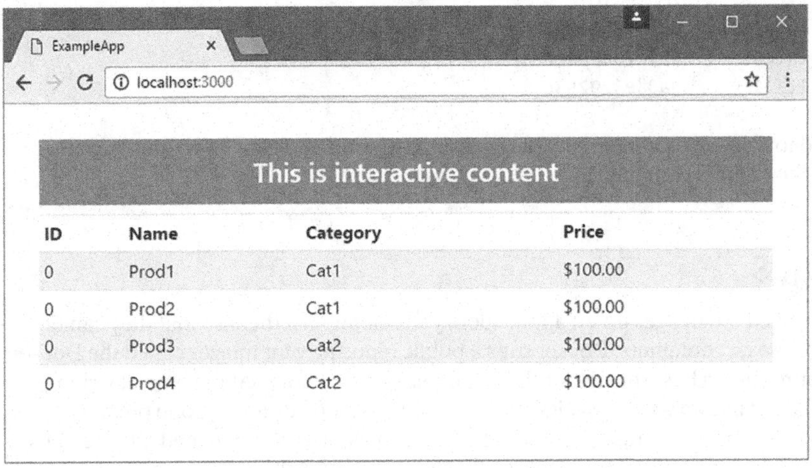

Figure 4-5. *Using the interactive shell in a Linux container*

INSTALLING AN EDITOR IN A LINUX CONTAINER

The most common task that requires interacting with a container is to use an editor to modify configuration files that are not created until the application has been started at least once. The base image for Linux containers for ASP.NET Core applications doesn't contain an editor, but you can add one using the following commands:

```
apt-get update
apt-get install vim
```

These commands download and install the venerable vi editor. If you have not used vi, then you can read about its commands at www.vim.org. That said, if you find yourself using a text editor, then ask yourself if you can solve the problem by changing the Docker file that creates the image from which the container has been created.

Creating Images from Modified Containers

Once you have modified a container, you can use the docker commit command to create a new image that incorporates the changes. Run the command in Listing 4-27 to create a new image that contains the changes made to the Razor view in Listing 4-26.

Listing 4-27. Committing Container Changes

```
docker commit exampleApp3000 apress/exampleapp:changed
```

This command creates a new variation of the apress/exampleapp image tagged as change. If you run the docker images command, you will see the new image has been added to the list.

```
REPOSITORY              TAG        IMAGE ID
apress/exampleapp       changed    00b418fa6548
apress/exampleapp       latest     827c2d48beca
microsoft/aspnetcore    1.1.1      da08e329253c
```

This image can be used to create new containers that contain the modified Razor view (and any other changes that were made to the original container).

Publishing Images

Once you have created and tested the images for an application, you can publish them so that they can be pulled to servers and used to create containers. Docker runs a public repository for images called the Docker Hub, which has been the source of the base images for the examples in this chapter. At the time of writing, you can create a free account that allows you to publish unlimited public repositories and one private repository. There are also paid-for accounts that allow more private repositories to be created. (There is also the Docker Store for paid-for software, but that isn't open to the public for publishing.)

■ **Note** For this section, you will need to visit http://hub.docker.com and create an account (the free account is sufficient).

Tagging the Images for Publication

The tags I have been using for the example images in this chapter start with apress, such as apress/exampleApp3000. When you publish an image to the Docker Hub, the first part of the tag must be the user name you used to create your account.

■ **Note** See https://docs.docker.com/registry/deploying for instructions for creating a private repository, which you can use to locally distribute images within your organization. This can be useful if you have images that contain sensitive information or if you have to conform to a policy that prohibits using third-party services.

For this section, I created a Docker Hub account with the user name of adamfreeman so that I can re-create the process that you will need to follow to set up the tags required for your own account. To publish your own images, replace adamfreeman in the commands that follow with your user name. Run the commands shown in Listing 4-28 to apply new tags to custom images so they have the right account information.

Listing 4-28. Adding Image Tags in Preparation for Publishing

```
docker tag apress/exampleapp:changed adamfreeman/exampleapp:changed
docker tag apress/exampleapp:latest adamfreeman/exampleapp:unchanged
```

The new tags create two variations of the image, changed and unchanged. These tags don't replace the original ones, which you can see using the `docker images` command, which will produce a result like this one:

```
REPOSITORY                 TAG          IMAGE ID         CREATED
apress/exampleapp          changed      b1af7e78f418     10 minutes ago
adamfreeman/exampleapp     changed      b1af7e78f418     10 minutes ago
apress/exampleapp          latest       452007c3b3dd     31 minutes ago
adamfreeman/exampleapp     unchanged    452007c3b3dd     31 minutes ago
microsoft/aspnetcore       1.1.1        da08e329253c     5 days ago
```

I like to remove the original tags to keep the list of images clean. Run the command shown in Listing 4-29 to remove the original tags, leaving just the new tags in place.

Listing 4-29. Removing Old Image Tags

```
docker rmi apress/exampleapp:changed apress/exampleapp:latest
```

Run the `docker images` command again and you will see that only the images with my account name are left.

```
REPOSITORY                 TAG          IMAGE ID         CREATED
adamfreeman/exampleapp     changed      b1af7e78f418     14 minutes ago
adamfreeman/exampleapp     unchanged    452007c3b3dd     35 minutes ago
microsoft/aspnetcore       1.1.1        da08e329253c     5 days ago
```

Authenticating with the Hub

The Docker Hub requires authentication before you can publish images to your account. Run the command shown in Listing 4-30 to authenticate yourself with the Docker Hub using the user name and password you used to create the account.

Listing 4-30. Authenticating with the Docker Hub

```
docker login -u <yourUsername> -p <yourPassword>
```

The `docker login` command uses the user name and password provided by the `-u` and `-p` arguments to perform authentication with the Hub. Once you have used the `docker login` command, subsequent commands sent to the Hub will include your authentication credentials.

Publishing the Images

Run the commands shown in Listing 4-31 to push your images to the Docker Hub.

Listing 4-31. Publishing Images to the Docker Hub

```
docker push adamfreeman/exampleapp:changed
docker push adamfreeman/exampleapp:unchanged
```

The first image can take a while to upload as the files it contains are transferred to the repository. The second image should be much quicker, since only the changes between the containers are needed.

If you omit the variation in the tag, then the images will be published as :latest. The Docker Hub does not enforce any kind of version control and doesn't automatically assign the most recent push request as the :latest image. For this reason, it is sensible to make an explicit push request that sets the image you want used by default. Run the commands shown in Listing 4-32 to tag and push a new image.

Listing 4-32. Tagging and Pushing the Default Variation for an Image

```
docker tag adamfreeman/exampleapp:unchanged adamfreeman/exampleapp:latest
docker push adamfreeman/exampleapp:latest
```

Finally, prevent anyone else using your account from publishing images by running the command shown in Listing 4-33 to log out of the Docker Hub. Further push requests will not work until the docker login command is used again.

Listing 4-33. Logging Out of the Docker Hub

```
docker logout
```

The images are now available in the Docker Hub. Log into hub.docker.com, locate your repository, and click the Tags section to see the images that have been published, as shown in Figure 4-6. You can use the Docker Hub web site to control access to your images and to provide additional information about them.

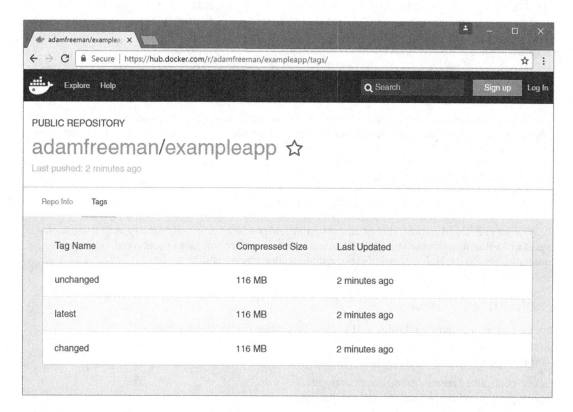

Figure 4-6. *Publishing images to the Docker Hub*

Creating Windows Containers

The images and containers created in the previous sections all rely on Linux as the execution platform. If you are using Linux as your development machine, the containers in the example have been running directly on your operating system using the Linux containers feature.

For Windows or macOS, Docker installs a Linux virtual machine that is used to execute containers. This blurs the lines between containers and virtual machines, but it does mean that a wider range of operating systems can be used to develop and test containers and that Windows and macOS users have access to the large library of images for containerized Linux applications that are available through Docker Hub.

But Linux isn't the only operating system that supports containers. Recent versions of Windows 10 and Windows Server 2016 also include container support that can be used to isolate and run Windows applications running on the Windows operating system.

From the perspective of ASP.NET Core MVC, support for Windows containers can be useful if you want to deploy your applications using Internet Information Services (IIS) or if your application depends on components that cannot run on Linux.

In the sections that follow, I explain how to create and test a Windows container. Creating a Windows container for an ASP.NET Core MVC application requires a similar process to the Linux equivalent but requires some important configuration changes.

■ **Note**   Windows containers can be created only using the Windows operating system and can be deployed only to Windows Server 2016. Linux containers are more widely supported, and there are more base images to work with. You should use Linux containers unless you have a specific need to containerize a Windows-only application.

Switching to Windows Containers

You must tell Docker that you want to switch from using Linux containers (the default) to using Windows containers. Right-click the Docker icon in the Windows task bar and select Switch To Windows Containers, as shown in Figure 4-7. (You don't have to perform this step when using Windows Server 2016, which supports only Windows containers.)

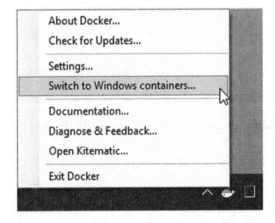

Figure 4-7. Switching to Windows containers

As part of the switch, you may be prompted to enable the Windows Containers feature, which will require a reboot.

If you have problems using Docker after you have switched between container types, then a reboot will usually solve the problem.

CREATING A WINDOWS SERVER VIRTUAL MACHINE

As I write this, the support for Windows containers on Windows 10 is at an early stage and has some problems, especially if you are using Hyper-V for conventional virtual machines alongside Docker. I found I got the best results by creating a regular Hyper-V virtual machine running Windows Server 2016 and using it to create and run my Docker Windows containers.

This technique requires switching on nested virtualization on the Windows 2016 virtual machine. Run the following command using PowerShell in the host operating system:

```
Set-VMProcessor -VMName <VMName> -ExposeVirtualizationExtensions $true
```

Replace `<VMName>` with the name assigned to the Windows Server 2016 virtual machine in Hyper-V. This command allows Docker to run in the Windows Server virtual machine and doesn't require switching between container types. See Chapter 3 for details of installing Docker in Windows Server 2016.

Creating a .NET Core Windows Image

Creating the image for a Windows container requires a different Docker file configuration. Create a file called `Dockerfile.windows` in the `ExampleApp` folder and add the commands shown in Listing 4-34.

Listing 4-34. The Contents of the Dockerfile.windows File in the ExampleApp Folder

```
FROM microsoft/dotnet:1.1.1-runtime-nanoserver

COPY dist /app

WORKDIR /app

EXPOSE 80/tcp

ENV ASPNETCORE_URLS http://+:80

ENTRYPOINT ["dotnet", "ExampleApp.dll"]
```

There are two differences between this Docker file and the one used for Linux containers. The first is that the FROM command specifies a different base image.

```
...
FROM microsoft/dotnet:1.1.1-runtime-nanoserver
...
```

The microsoft/dotnet image is the official image for .NET Core and is available in variations that provide different versions of .NET, a choice between the runtime or the SDK, and both Linux and Windows options. The 1.1.1-runtime-nanoserver variation specified in the listing contains the version 1.1.1 of the .NET Core runtime and is based on Windows. (Windows Nano Server is a minimal installation of Windows that is suitable for use in containers.)

■ **Tip** You can see the full set of variations and versions of the microsoft/dotnet image at the Docker Hub.

The second change is the addition of this ENV command:

```
...
ENV ASPNETCORE_URLS http://+:80
...
```

The ENV command sets an environment variable in the container. In this case, the command sets the value of the ASPNETCORE_URLS environment variable, which sets the port that the Kestrel server listens on to 80. The base image I used for the Linux containers includes this environment variable. Setting the port isn't a requirement but ensures that I can create and use Windows containers using the same Docker commands I used for the Linux containers earlier in the chapter.

Creating the Image and the Container

The process for creating an image and container for Windows is the same as for Linux. Run the commands in Listing 4-35 in the ExampleApp folder to publish the application and use the new Docker file to create an image.

Listing 4-35. Creating an Image for a Windows Container

```
dotnet restore
dotnet publish --framework netcoreapp1.1 --configuration Release --output dist
docker build . -t apress/exampleapp:windows -f Dockerfile.windows
```

To differentiate between the Linux and Windows containers for the example applications, I used the -t argument to the docker build command to specify a tag for the image that contains a variation so that the name of the image is apress/exampleapp:windows.

■ **Tip** If you see an unknown blob error when you run the command in Listing 4-35, then use the task bar icon to check that Docker has switched to Windows containers. If you had to reboot to enable containers, then Docker may have reset to Linux containers when it started.

Run the command shown in Listing 4-36 to create and start a new container using the Windows image.

Listing 4-36. Creating and Starting the Windows Container

```
docker run -p 7000:80 --name exampleAppWin apress/exampleapp:windows
```

Type Control+C to detach the command prompt and leave the container running. (The messages written out indicate that Control+C will terminate the application, but this is a message from Kestrel, the ASP.NET Core server, which doesn't receive the keystrokes. When working with Docker, it can be easy to confuse the container with the application that is running inside of it.)

Testing the Windows Container

At the time of writing, there is a problem with Windows containers that means they cannot be tested by requesting the mapped port through localhost, as I did for the Linux containers. This is a result of the way that the networking for containers is set up by Docker.

If you have another machine (or virtual machine available), then you can test the Windows container using the host operating system's IP address and the mapped port, which is 7000 in this example.

If you have only your development machine, then you can test using the IP address assigned to the container. Run the command in Listing 4-37 to get detailed information about the Windows container.

Listing 4-37. Inspecting a Container

```
docker inspect exampleAppWin
```

The output will include a Networks/nat section that contains an IP address, like this:

```
...
"Networks": {
    "nat": {
        "IPAMConfig": null,
        "Links": null,
        "Aliases": null,
        "NetworkID": "d41dba49b91fcd7fdfc5f7f520976db353",
        "EndpointID": "ca60ef2b19f591a0cf03b27407142cea7",
        "Gateway": "",
        "IPAddress": " 172.29.172.154",
        "IPPrefixLen": 16,
        "IPv6Gateway": "",
        "GlobalIPv6Address": "",
        "GlobalIPv6PrefixLen": 0,
        "MacAddress": "00:15:5d:68:1f:22"
    }
}
...
```

Use this address to send an HTTP request to the container, using the port used by the application (and not the port mapped to the host operating system outside the container).

You may see a different IP address in the output from the docker inspect command, but for me, the URL that will test the container is http://172.29.172.154:80, producing the result shown in Figure 4-8.

■ **Note**   The microsoft/dotnet image doesn't contain the natively compiled packages that are included in the microsoft/aspnetcore image that I used for the Linux image earlier in the chapter. This doesn't stop the container from running, but it does mean it takes slightly longer to process the first request.

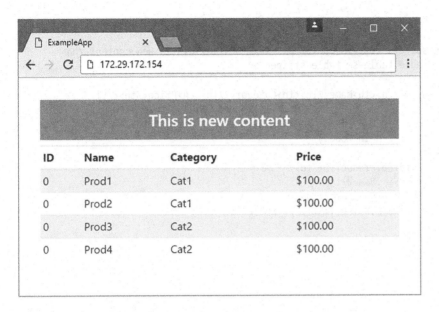

Figure 4-8. *Testing the Windows container*

Executing Commands in Windows Containers

If you are using a Windows container, then you can invoke commands inside the container with PowerShell. Open a second PowerShell and run the command shown in Listing 4-38 to execute a command inside the Windows container.

Listing 4-38. Executing a Command in a Windows Container

```
docker exec exampleAppWin PowerShell cat /app/Views/Home/Index.cshtml
```

This command returns the contents of the Razor view, as follows:

```
@model IEnumerable<ExampleApp.Models.Product>
@{
    Layout = null;
}
<!DOCTYPE html>
<html>
<head>
    <meta name="viewport" content="width=device-width" />
    <title>ExampleApp</title>
    <link rel="stylesheet" href="~/lib/bootstrap/dist/css/bootstrap.min.css" />
</head>
```

```
<body>
    <div class="m-1 p-1">
        <h4 class="bg-success text-xs-center p-1 text-white">This is new content</h4>
        <table class="table table-sm table-striped">
            <thead>
                <tr><th>ID</th><th>Name</th><th>Category</th><th>Price</th></tr>
            </thead>
            <tbody>
                @foreach (var p in Model) {
                    <tr>
                        <td>@p.ProductID</td>
                        <td>@p.Name</td>
                        <td>@p.Category</td>
                        <td>$@p.Price.ToString("F2")</td>
                    </tr>

                }
            </tbody>
        </table>
    </div>
</body>
</html>
```

Interacting with Windows Containers

You can also interact with a container using PowerShell directly. Run the command shown in Listing 4-39 to interactively execute PowerShell inside the Windows container.

Listing 4-39. Starting a Shell in a Windows Container

```
docker exec -it exampleAppWin PowerShell
```

Once the shell has started, use the commands in Listing 4-40 to modify the contents of the Razor view.

Listing 4-40. Modifying the Razor View in PowerShell

```
cd C:\app\Views\Home
(Get-Content .\Index.cshtml).replace("This is new content", "Essential (Windows) Docker") |
Set-Content Index.cshtml
exit
```

The first command changes the working directory, and the second command replaces the phrase This is new content with Essential (Windows) Docker. The final command exits the shell. If you use the browser to send a request to the browser (as explained in the "*Creating Windows Containers*" section), you will see the effect of the change, as illustrated by Figure 4-9.

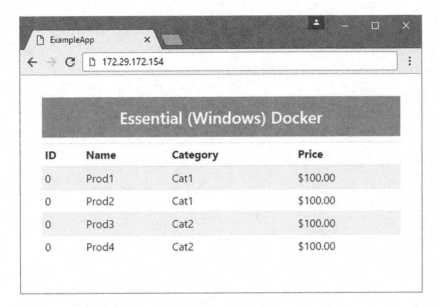

Figure 4-9. *Using the interactive shell in a Windows container*

Summary

In this chapter, I demonstrated how to create and manage Docker images and containers. I showed you how to create Windows and Linux containers, how to modify containers and use the changes to create new images, and how to publish images to the Docker Hub. In the next chapter, I explain how Docker deals with application data and how multiple containers can be connected together using software-defined networks.

CHAPTER 5

■ ■ ■

Docker Volumes and Networks

In this chapter, I describe two Docker features that are designed to deal with more complex applications and, specifically, applications that are made up of multiple containers.

The first feature, called *volumes*, separates the data files that are generated by an application or a database from the rest of the container's storage, which makes it easier to replace or upgrade a container. The second feature, known as *software-defined networks*, allows containers to communicate, which makes it easier to scale an application to handle larger workloads. Table 5-1 puts volumes and software-defined networks in context.

Table 5-1. *Putting Docker Volumes and Software-Defined Networks in Context*

Question	Answer
What are they?	Volumes allow important data to exist outside of the container, which means you can replace a container without losing the data that it created.
	Software-defined networks are Internet Protocol networks created by Docker that allow the applications in containers to communicate.
Why are they useful?	Volumes make it possible to delete a container without also deleting the data it contains, which allows containers to be changed or upgraded without losing user data.
	Software-defined networks make it possible to create more complex applications that span multiple containers, making it easier to introduce common components like databases.
How are they used?	These features are managed through the docker volume and docker network commands. Volumes and software-defined networks must be prepared before the containers that use them are created.
Are there any pitfalls or limitations?	Working out which volumes are required by base images can be a difficult process.
	Software-defined networks only connect containers on a single server unless a Docker cluster is used (as described in Chapter 7).
Are there any alternatives?	There are no alternatives to these features, but you require them for every project. Volumes are not required if a containerized application doesn't generate data that you need to save when the container is removed. Software-defined networks are not required if your containers do not need to communicate.

© Adam Freeman 2017
A. Freeman, *Essential Docker for ASP.NET Core MVC*, DOI 10.1007/978-1-4842-2778-7_5

Table 5-2 summarizes the chapter.

Table 5-2. *Chapter Summary*

Problem	Solution	Listing
Ensure that data files are preserved when a container is deleted	Create a volume and use it to provide the contents of a directory in the container's file system	1–11, 13–17
Determine whether a container uses a volume	Use the docker inspect command	12
Add a database to an ASP.NET Core MVC application	Create and apply a volume to the database container and configure Entity Framework Core to connect to the database in the container	18–29
Connect containers together	Create a software-defined network and connect containers to it	30–34
Connect a container to a software-defined network	Use the --network argument when creating the container or use the docker network connect command	35–39
Distribute work between containers connected to a software-defined network	Use a load balancer that directs requests to containers using the Docker DNS feature	40–41

Preparing for This Chapter

This chapter depends on the ExampleApp MVC project created in Chapter 3. If you don't want to work through the process of creating the example, you can get the project as part of the free source code download for which there is a link on the apress.com page for this book.

If you are a Windows user and you followed the examples in the previous chapter to create Windows containers, then you must return to working with Linux containers. Right-click the Docker icon in the task bar and select Switch to Linux Containers from the pop-up menu.

To ensure that there is no conflict with earlier examples, run the command shown in Listing 5-1 to remove the containers created in the previous chapter.

Listing 5-1. Removing the Containers

```
docker rm -f $(docker ps -aq)
```

Working with Volumes

There are two kinds of file associated with an application: the files required to run the application and the data files that application generates as it runs, which are typically produced as a result of user actions. In the world of Docker, these two types of files are handled differently.

The files required to run the application are part of the Docker container for an application. When Docker processes the instructions in a Docker file, it builds up the image that forms the template for containers. For an ASP.NET Core MVC application, this means that containers include the .NET Core runtime, the ASP.NET Core packages, the custom C# classes, the Bootstrap CSS stylesheet, the Razor view, and all of the configuration files. Without these files, a containerized MVC application would not be able to run.

Data files are not included in containers. One of the key benefits of using containers is that they are easy to create and destroy. When a container is destroyed, the files in its file system are deleted as well, which would be disastrous for data files because they would be lost forever.

Docker provides a feature called *volumes* to manage application data, and in the following sections, I explain how volumes work, demonstrate the tools that are available for working with them, and show you a common type of application that uses volumes: a database.

Demonstrating the Problem

Volumes can be confusing, and the best place to start is to demonstrate what happens when they are not used. Create a file called Dockerfile.volumes in the ExampleApp folder and add the commands shown in Listing 5-2.

Listing 5-2. The Contents of the Dockerfile.volumes File in the ExampleApp Folder

```
FROM alpine:3.4

WORKDIR /data

ENTRYPOINT (test -e message.txt && echo "File Exists" \
        || (echo "Creating File..." \
        && echo Hello, Docker $(date '+%X') > message.txt)) && cat message.txt
```

This Docker file uses the minimal Alpine Linux distribution as its base. To simulate an application that generates data, the ENTRYPOINT command creates a data file called the /data/message.txt file that contains a message and a timestamp.

The data file isn't created until the container is started and won't be part of the image that is created from the Docker file, similar to the content of a database in a real application.

Run the commands in Listing 5-3 from the ExampleApp folder to build an image from the Docker file and use that image to create and start a new container.

Listing 5-3. Creating an Image and a Container

```
docker build . -t apress/vtest -f Dockerfile.volumes
docker run --name vtest apress/vtest
```

The container will produce the following output when Docker starts it, although you will see a different timestamp:

```
...
Creating File...
Hello, Docker 20:21:50
...
```

The container exits once it has written out the message, which shows that the /data/message.txt data file has been created and that it has been timestamped at 20:21:50.

Because I have not set up a volume for the data file, it has become part of the container's file system. The file system is persistent, which you can see by running the command in Listing 5-4 to start the same container again.

Listing 5-4. Restarting the Container

```
docker start -a vtest
```

This time you will see output like this:

```
...
File Exists
Hello, Docker 20:21:50
...
```

The output indicates that the /data/message.txt file already exists and has the same timestamp.

The problems with data files occur when a container is deleted. As you will learn in later chapters, Docker containers are created and destroyed often, either to reflect a change in the workload or to deploy a new version of the application. Run the command shown in Listing 5-5 to remove the container.

Listing 5-5. Deleting a Container

```
docker rm -f vtest
```

Docker will delete the container, and the /data/message.txt file is lost. To confirm that this is the case, run the command shown in Listing 5-6 to create and run another container from the same image.

Listing 5-6. Replacing the Container

```
docker run --name vtest apress/vtest
```

The output from the container shows that a new data file has been created.

```
...
Creating File...
Hello, Docker 20:53:26
...
```

To state the obvious, deleting data files in a real application has serious consequences and should be avoided.

Managing Data with a Docker Volume

Docker volumes solve the data file problem by keeping data files outside the container while still making them accessible to the application that runs inside it. There are three steps to using a volume, which I describe in the sections that follow.

Step 1: Updating the Docker File

The first step to applying a volume is to add a command to the Docker file, as shown in Listing 5-7.

Listing 5-7. Declaring a Volume in the Dockerfile.volumes File in the ExampleApp Folder

```
FROM alpine:3.4

VOLUME /data

WORKDIR /data
```

```
ENTRYPOINT (test -e message.txt && echo "File Exists" \
       || (echo "Creating File..." \
       && echo Hello, Docker $(date '+%X') > message.txt)) && cat message.txt
```

The VOLUME command tells Docker that any files stored in /data should be stored in a volume, putting them outside the regular container file system. The important point to note is that the application running in the container won't know that the files in the /data directory are special: they will be read and written just like any other file in the container's file system.

Save the changes to the Docker file and run the command shown in Listing 5-8 in the ExampleApp folder to re-create the image.

Listing 5-8. Updating the Image to Use a Volume

```
docker build . -t apress/vtest -f Dockerfile.volumes
```

Step 2: Creating the Volume

The second step is to create the volume that will hold the data files. Run the command shown in Listing 5-9 to create the volume that will be used to store the data files for the example application.

Listing 5-9. Creating a Volume

```
docker volume create --name testdata
```

The docker volume create command is used to create a new volume and assign it a name, which is testdata in this case. The volume is a self-contained file system that will provide the contents for one directory in the container's file system. Since the volume isn't part of the container, the files it contains are not deleted when the container is destroyed.

Step 3: Creating the Container

The third and final step is to tell Docker which volume should be used by the container. Run the command shown in Listing 5-10 in the ExampleApp folder to create a container that uses the testdata volume created in Listing 5-9 to provide the contents for the /data directory configured in Listing 5-7.

Listing 5-10. Associating a Volume with a Container

```
docker run --name vtest2 -v testdata:/data apress/vtest
```

The -v argument tells Docker that any data the container creates in the /data directory should be stored in the testdata volume. The volume appears like a regular directory to the application, which creates the data file like it did before. The output from the command in Listing 5-10 will indicate that a data file has been created, like this:

```
...
Creating File...
Hello, Docker 21:48:20
...
```

Nothing has changed as far as the application is concerned. The simple script I set up in the Docker file's ENTRYPOINT command checks to see whether there is a message.txt file in the /data directory. Volumes are empty when they are first created, which means the application didn't find the file and created it.

The effect of using the volume is apparent only when the container is destroyed and replaced. Run the commands shown in Listing 5-11 to remove the existing container and create and run its replacement.

Listing 5-11. Testing the Volume

```
docker rm -f vtest2
docker run --name vtest2 -v testdata:/data apress/vtest
```

Once again, the -v argument is used with the docker run command to tell Docker to use the testdata volume to provide the contents for the /data directory. This time, when the ENTRYPOINT script looks for the /data/message.txt file, it discovers the one created by the previous container, which has survived because the volume was unaffected when the container was destroyed. You will see the output that shows that the file didn't have to be created, similar to this:

```
...
File Exists
Hello, Docker 21:48:20
...
```

Determining Whether an Image Uses Volumes

There are two ways to check to see whether a Docker image relies on volumes. The first—and most obvious—is to look at the Docker file that was used to create the image. Many publicly available images on Docker include a link to a GitHub repository, where you can easily inspect the Docker file and see whether it contains any VOLUME commands. Remember to consider the base image as well when reading Docker files.

The other approach is to examine an image directly, which is useful if you don't have access to the Docker file. Run the command in Listing 5-12 to examine the image used in the previous section.

Listing 5-12. Examining a Docker Image

```
docker inspect apress/vtest
```

The response from the docker inspect command is a JSON description of the image, which includes information about the volumes that are used. For the example image, the response from the docker inspect command will include the following:

```
...
"Volumes": {
    "/data": {}
},
...
```

The Volumes section of the description lists the volumes that the images uses and that can be configured using the -v argument to the docker run or docker create commands.

Adding a Database to the Example Application

Most ASP.NET Core MVC applications rely on a database, which means there are database files that should be stored in a volume so they are not deleted when the database container is destroyed.

However, since the contents of a volume are not included in images, even when the `docker commit` command is used, some special measures are required to ensure that the application's data model schema is created and any seed data applied when the database is first started.

In the sections that follow, I explain how to add a database to the example application, including the steps required to use a volume to contain the data files.

There are lots of database servers available, but the most common choice for containerized ASP.NET Core applications tends to be MySQL, which runs well in Linux containers and has good-quality support in Entity Framework Core (EF Core), which is the object/relational mapping framework used in most ASP.NET Core applications.

To make sure that previous examples don't interfere with the containers in this chapter, run the command shown in Listing 5-13 to remove all the Docker containers.

Listing 5-13. Removing the Existing Docker Containers

```
docker rm -f $(docker ps -aq)
```

SELECTING A DATABASE SERVER

The most common database server choice for ASP.NET Core MVC when Docker isn't being used is Microsoft SQL Server. At the time of writing, the use of SQL Server in Docker is at an early stage. SQL Server runs well in Windows, but Docker support for Windows Containers is still new and has some rough edges. Microsoft has released a preview of SQL Server running on Linux, which will be ideally suited for Docker Linux containers when it stabilizes, but, at least as I write this, the Linux version is not ready for production use. When Microsoft releases the final version, I will post an updated example to this book's source code repository, for which you can find a link on the `apress.com` page for this book.

Pulling and Inspecting the Database Image

When adding a new component to a containerized application, it is important to start by inspecting the image to see how it uses volumes so that you know how to configure the containers that you create. If you skip this step, everything will be fine until you remove a container and find that the data files it contains are removed as well.

Run the commands shown in Listing 5-14 to pull the image for MySQL from the Docker Hub and inspect it.

Listing 5-14. Pulling and Inspecting the MySQL Docker Hub Image

```
docker pull mysql:8.0.0
docker inspect mysql:8.0.0
```

Examine the output from the `docker inspect` command and locate the Volumes section, which will look like this:

```
...
"Volumes": {
    "/var/lib/mysql": {}
},
...
```

This tells you that the `mysql:8.0.0` image uses a volume for its `/var/lib/mysql` directory, which is where MySQL stores its data files.

■ **Tip**   Don't be tempted to create a Docker image that contains your ASP.NET Core MVC application and the database so they can run in a single container. The convention for Docker is to use a separate container for each component in an application, which makes it easier to upgrade or replace parts of the application and allows a more flexible approach to scaling up the application once it is deployed. You won't benefit from Docker's most useful features if you create a monolithic container that includes all your application components.

Creating the Volume and Container

To prepare for the database container, run the command shown in Listing 5-15 to create the Docker volume called `productdata` that will be used to store the database data files.

Listing 5-15. Creating a Volume for the Database Container

```
docker volume create --name productdata
```

Run the command shown in Listing 5-16 to create and start a new MySQL container that uses the volume to provide the container with the contents of the `/var/lib/mysql` directory. (Enter the command on a single line.)

Listing 5-16. Creating and Starting a MySQL Container

```
docker run -d --name mysql -v productdata:/var/lib/mysql
   -e MYSQL_ROOT_PASSWORD=mysecret -e bind-address=0.0.0.0 mysql:8.0.0
```

As explained in Chapter 4, the `docker run` command creates a container and starts it in a single step. Table 5-3 shows the arguments used to configure the MySQL container.

Table 5-3. *The Arguments Used to Configure the MySQL Container*

Name	Description
-d	This argument tells Docker to run the container in the background without attaching to it to display the output.
--name	This argument is used to assign the name `mysql` to the container, which makes it easier to refer to in other Docker commands.
-e MYSQL_ROOT_PASSWORD	This argument sets an environment variable. In this case, the MySQL container uses the `MYSQL_ROOT_PASSWORD` environment variable to set the password required to connect to the database. I have set the password to `mysecret` for the example application, but you should use a more secure password for real projects.
-e bind-address	This argument sets an environment variable. This environment variable ensures that MySQL accepts requests on all network interfaces.
-v productdata:/var/lib/mysql	This argument tells Docker to use a volume called `productdata` to provide the contents of the container's `/var/lib/mysql` directory.

Run the command shown in Listing 5-17 to monitor the database startup.

Listing 5-17. Monitoring the Database Startup

```
docker logs -f mysql
```

It will take a while for MySql to initialize, during which time it will write out log messages. Many of these messages will be warnings that can be ignored. The messages will stop once the database is ready, and one of the last messages shown will be like the following, which indicates that the database is ready to accept network connections:

```
...
08:42:00.729460Z 0 [Note] mysqld: ready for connections.
...
```

Subsequent initializations will be much faster because they will be able to use the files that have been created in the productdata volume. Once the database is running, type Control+C to stop monitoring the output and leave the database running in its container in the background.

Preparing the Example Application

Data for an ASP.NET Core MVC application is typically provided by the Entity Framework Core (known as EF Core), which is the ASP.NET object/relational mapping framework. Edit the ExampleApp.csproj file to add the packages shown in Listing 5-18.

Listing 5-18. Adding Packages in the ExampleApp.csproj File in the ExampleApp Folder

```
<Project Sdk="Microsoft.NET.Sdk.Web">

  <PropertyGroup>
    <TargetFramework>netcoreapp1.1</TargetFramework>
  </PropertyGroup>

  <ItemGroup>
    <PackageReference Include="Microsoft.AspNetCore" Version="1.1.1" />
    <PackageReference Include="Microsoft.AspNetCore.Mvc" Version="1.1.2" />
    <PackageReference Include="Microsoft.AspNetCore.StaticFiles" Version="1.1.1" />
    <PackageReference Include="Microsoft.Extensions.Logging.Debug" Version="1.1.1" />
    <PackageReference Include="Microsoft.VisualStudio.Web.BrowserLink"
        Version="1.1.0" />

    <PackageReference Include="Microsoft.EntityFrameworkCore" Version="1.1.1" />
    <PackageReference Include="Microsoft.EntityFrameworkCore.Tools"
        Version="1.1.0" />
    <PackageReference Include="Pomelo.EntityFrameworkCore.MySql" Version="1.1.0" />
    <DotNetCliToolReference Include="Microsoft.EntityFrameworkCore.Tools.DotNet"
        Version="1.0.0" />
  </ItemGroup>
</Project>
```

The new packages add the EF Core packages from Microsoft and the Pomelo.EntityFrameworkCore. MySql package, which contains a database provider for MySql. There is an official database provider available from the MySql project, but I find that the Pomelo provider used in this chapter gets updated more rapidly and is easier to work with.

Save the changes to the ExampleApp.csproj file and run the command shown in Listing 5-19 in the ExampleApp folder to download the new packages.

Listing 5-19. Updating the Example Project Packages

```
dotnet restore
```

Creating the Repository Class

At the moment, the example application has dummy data that is provided by a placeholder implementation of the repository interface, which I put in place in Chapter 3 just to get the application started.

Replacing the dummy data with data accessed through EF Core requires a database context class. Add a file called ProductDbContext.cs to the ExampleApp/Models folder and add the code shown in Listing 5-20.

Listing 5-20. The Contents of the ProductDbContext.cs File in the ExampleApp/Models Folder

```
using Microsoft.EntityFrameworkCore;

namespace ExampleApp.Models {

    public class ProductDbContext : DbContext {

        public ProductDbContext(DbContextOptions<ProductDbContext> options)
            : base(options) {
        }

        public DbSet<Product> Products { get; set; }
    }
}
```

The ProductDbContext class will provide access to the Product objects in the database through its Products property. To provide access to the data elsewhere in the application, add a file called ProductRepository.cs to the ExampleApp/Models folder and add the code shown in Listing 5-21.

Listing 5-21. The Contents of the ProductRepository.cs File in the ExampleApp/Models Folder

```
using System.Linq;

namespace ExampleApp.Models {

    public class ProductRepository : IRepository {
        private ProductDbContext context;

        public ProductRepository(ProductDbContext ctx) {
            context = ctx;
        }

        public IQueryable<Product> Products => context.Products;
    }
}
```

This is a simple repository that exposes the Product objects in the database through a Products property. In a real project, the repository would also provide methods to create and modify objects, but I have omitted these to keep the focus on Docker.

To define seed data that will be added to the application when the database is empty, create a file called SeedData.cs in the ExampleApp/Models folder and add the code shown in Listing 5-22.

Listing 5-22. The Contents of the SeedData.cs File in the ExampleApp/Models Folder

```
using Microsoft.AspNetCore.Builder;
using Microsoft.EntityFrameworkCore;
using Microsoft.Extensions.DependencyInjection;
using System.Linq;

namespace ExampleApp.Models {

    public static class SeedData {

        public static void EnsurePopulated(IApplicationBuilder app) {
            EnsurePopulated(
                app.ApplicationServices.GetRequiredService<ProductDbContext>());
        }

        public static void EnsurePopulated(ProductDbContext context) {
            System.Console.WriteLine("Applying Migrations...");
            context.Database.Migrate();

            if (!context.Products.Any()) {

                System.Console.WriteLine("Creating Seed Data...");
                context.Products.AddRange(
                    new Product("Kayak", "Watersports", 275),
                    new Product("Lifejacket", "Watersports", 48.95m),
                    new Product("Soccer Ball", "Soccer", 19.50m),
                    new Product("Corner Flags", "Soccer", 34.95m),
                    new Product("Stadium", "Soccer", 79500),
                    new Product("Thinking Cap", "Chess", 16),
                    new Product("Unsteady Chair", "Chess", 29.95m),
                    new Product("Human Chess Board", "Chess", 75),
                    new Product("Bling-Bling King", "Chess", 1200)
                );
                context.SaveChanges();
            } else {
                System.Console.WriteLine("Seed Data Not Required...");
            }
        }
    }
}
```

The static EnsurePopulated method creates a database context object and uses it to add Product objects to the database. The most important statement in the SeedData class is this one:

```
...
context.Database.Migrate();
...
```

EF Core manages the schema of the database using a feature called *migrations*, which are usually applied to the database through a command-line tool. This doesn't work when using Docker because it is difficult to perform manual configuration steps when deploying an application. Instead, the Database.Migrate method is called during application startup to apply any pending migrations to the database. This ensures that the database schema is created without needing any command-line intervention, but, as you will learn, different techniques are required for production applications, as described in later chapters.

Configuring the Application

To configure the application and enable the EF Core services, make the modifications shown in Listing 5-23 to the Startup class.

Listing 5-23. Configuring the Application in the Startup.cs File in the ExampleApp Folder

```
using ExampleApp.Models;
using Microsoft.AspNetCore.Builder;
using Microsoft.AspNetCore.Hosting;
using Microsoft.Extensions.DependencyInjection;
using Microsoft.Extensions.Logging;
using Microsoft.Extensions.Configuration;
using Microsoft.EntityFrameworkCore;

namespace ExampleApp {
    public class Startup {

        private IConfigurationRoot Configuration;

        public Startup(IHostingEnvironment env) {
            Configuration = new ConfigurationBuilder()
                .SetBasePath(env.ContentRootPath)
                .AddEnvironmentVariables()
                .Build();
        }

        public void ConfigureServices(IServiceCollection services) {

            var host = Configuration["DBHOST"] ?? "localhost";
            var port = Configuration["DBPORT"] ?? "3306";
            var password = Configuration["DBPASSWORD"] ?? "mysecret";

            services.AddDbContext<ProductDbContext>(options =>
                options.UseMySql($"server={host};userid=root;pwd={password};"
                    + $"port={port};database=products"));

            services.AddSingleton<IConfiguration>(Configuration);
            services.AddTransient<IRepository, ProductRepository>();
            services.AddMvc();
        }
```

```
public void Configure(IApplicationBuilder app,
        IHostingEnvironment env, ILoggerFactory loggerFactory) {

    loggerFactory.AddConsole();
    app.UseDeveloperExceptionPage();
    app.UseStatusCodePages();
    app.UseStaticFiles();
    app.UseMvcWithDefaultRoute();

    SeedData.EnsurePopulated(app);
    }
  }
}
```

In conventional MVC projects, the connection string for the database is defined in a JSON configuration file, but when working with containers, it is simpler to use environment variables because they can be easily specified when a container is started so that you don't have to rebuild the image and re-create the containers each time there is a configuration change. In this example, the host name, TCP port, and password are configured by reading the value of environment variables called DBHOST, DBPORT, and DBPASSWORD. There are default values for these configuration settings that will be used if the environment variables are not defined.

Creating the Database Migration

The next step is to create the initial Entity Framework Core migration that will define the schema for the application. This uses the EF Core Code First feature, which generates database schemas automatically from the data model classes in an ASP.NET Core application. Run the command shown in Listing 5-24 from the ExampleApp folder to create the migration.

Listing 5-24. Creating the Initial Database Migration

```
dotnet ef migrations add Initial
```

If you are using Visual Studio, you can open the Package Manager Console (available in the Tools ➤ NuGet Package Manager menu) and run the PowerShell command shown in Listing 5-25 instead.

Listing 5-25. Creating the Database Migrations Using the Visual Studio Package Manager Console

```
Add-Migration Initial
```

Regardless of which command you use, Entity Framework Core will create an Example/Migrations folder that contains C# classes that will be used create the database schema. (If you see an error telling you that the term Add-Migration is not recognized, then restart Visual Studio and load the example project again. Once the project has loaded, you should be able to run the Add-Migration command from the Package Manager Console.)

■ **Note** You might be used to running the `dotnet ef database update` or `Update-Database` command at this point, but these are not helpful when working with Docker. Instead, the MVC application has been configured to apply the migration when it starts, as shown in Listing 5-23 or by using the techniques described in later chapters.

Changing the View

Earlier examples modified the banner message in the Razor view to indicate when content has been altered. Return the view to a simpler message that displays just the value provided by the controller, as shown in Listing 5-26.

Listing 5-26. Resetting the Contents of the Index.cshtml File in the ExampleApp/Views/Home Folder

```
@model IEnumerable<ExampleApp.Models.Product>
@{
    Layout = null;
}
<!DOCTYPE html>
<html>
<head>
    <meta name="viewport" content="width=device-width" />
    <title>ExampleApp</title>
    <link rel="stylesheet" href="~/lib/bootstrap/dist/css/bootstrap.min.css" />
</head>
<body>
    <div class="m-1 p-1">
        <h4 class="bg-success text-xs-center p-1 text-white">@ViewBag.Message</h4>
        <table class="table table-sm table-striped">
            <thead>
                <tr><th>ID</th><th>Name</th><th>Category</th><th>Price</th></tr>
            </thead>
            <tbody>
                @foreach (var p in Model) {
                    <tr>
                        <td>@p.ProductID</td>
                        <td>@p.Name</td>
                        <td>@p.Category</td>
                        <td>$@p.Price.ToString("F2")</td>
                    </tr>

                }
            </tbody>
        </table>
    </div>
</body>
</html>
```

Creating the MVC Application Image

The final preparatory step is to update the image for the MVC application so that it includes the code changes to support the database, the Entity Framework Core packages, and the initial migration that will create the database schema and apply the seed data. Run the commands shown in Listing 5-27 in the ExampleApp folder to publish the application and create a new Docker image.

Listing 5-27. Updating the MVC Application Image

```
dotnet publish --framework netcoreapp1.1 --configuration Release --output dist
docker build . -t apress/exampleapp -f Dockerfile
```

The dotnet publish command prepares the MVC application for containerization and writes all of the files that it requires into the dist folder, as explained in Chapter 4. The docker build command uses the Dockerfile to generate a new image, which is assigned the apress/exampleapp tag.

Testing the Application

All that remains is to test the new image by creating a container for the ASP.NET Core MVC application and ensuring that it can communicate with the MySQL database, which is already running in its own container, created in Listing 5-16. This testing requires a little work, but it provides some useful insights into how Docker works.

When you start a container, Docker connects it to an internal virtual network and assigns it an Internet Protocol (IP) address so that it can communicate with the host server and with other containers on the same network. This is the entry point for a key Docker feature that I describe in the next section of this chapter (known as *software-defined networks*).

To have the MVC container talk to the database, I need to know the IP address that Docker assigned to the MySQL container. Run the command shown in Listing 5-28 to examine the configuration of the Docker virtual network.

Listing 5-28. Examining the Docker Virtual Network

```
docker network inspect bridge
```

The response from this command will show you how Docker has configured the virtual network and will include a Containers section that shows the containers that are connected to the network and the IP addresses that are assigned to them.

There should be only one container, and its Name field will be mysql. Make a note of the IPv4Address field, as follows:

```
...
"Containers": {
    "72753560ccb4d876bdeaad36e0b39354a08e90ad30ac1a78b20aad3e52b7a101": {
        "Name": "mysql",
        "EndpointID": "04f18afbf953a030ddfbbadf4a8f86c1dbf6c6a6736449326",
        "MacAddress": "02:42:ac:11:00:02",
        "IPv4Address": "172.17.0.2/16",
        "IPv6Address": ""
    }
},
...
```

This is the IP address that Docker has assigned to the container. For me, the address is `172.17.0.2`, but you may see a different address. This is the IP address that the MVC application must use in its database connection to communicate with MySQL. This address can be provided to the application through the `DBHOST` environment variable, which is read by the additions to the MVC application's `Startup` class that I made in Listing 5-22.

Run the commands shown in Listing 5-29 to create and start an MVC container in the background and then to monitor its output. Make sure you use the IP address that has been assigned to the MySQL container on your system, shown in the output you received from the command in Listing 5-29.

Listing 5-29. Creating and Starting a New MVC Application Container

```
docker run -d --name productapp -p 3000:80 -e DBHOST=172.17.0.2 apress/exampleapp
docker logs -f productapp
```

As the MVC application starts up, you will see messages that show that Entity Framework Core has applied its migrations to the database, which ensures that the schema is created and that the seed data is added.

```
...
Applying Migrations...
info: Microsoft.EntityFrameworkCore.Migrations.Internal.Migrator[12]
      Applying migration '20161215112411_Initial'.
Creating Seed Data...

...SQL statements omitted for brevity...

Hosting environment: Production
Content root path: /app
Now listening on: http://+:80
Application started. Press Ctrl+C to shut down.
...
```

The `docker run` command in Listing 5-29 maps port 3000 on the host operating system to port 80 in the container, which is the port that Kestrel is using to receive HTTP requests for the ASP.NET Core runtime. To test the application, open a new browser tab and request the URL `http://localhost:3000`. The browser will send an HTTP request that Docker will receive and direct to port 80 in the MVC container, producing the response shown in Figure 5-1.

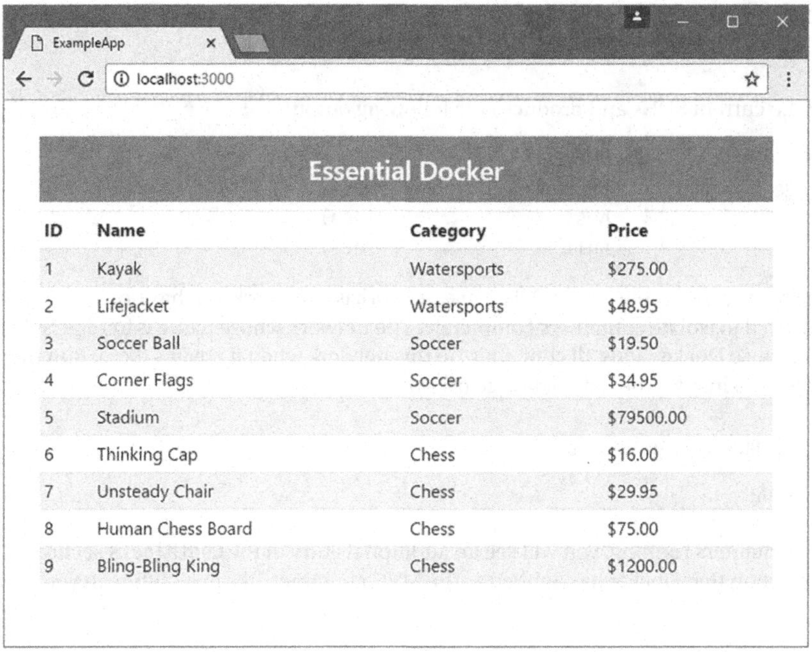

ID	Name	Category	Price
1	Kayak	Watersports	$275.00
2	Lifejacket	Watersports	$48.95
3	Soccer Ball	Soccer	$19.50
4	Corner Flags	Soccer	$34.95
5	Stadium	Soccer	$79500.00
6	Thinking Cap	Chess	$16.00
7	Unsteady Chair	Chess	$29.95
8	Human Chess Board	Chess	$75.00
9	Bling-Bling King	Chess	$1200.00

Figure 5-1. *Testing the example application*

The data displayed in the response from the MVC application was obtained from the MySQL server using Entity Framework Core. The Docker network allowed the EF Core to open a network connection to the MySQL container and use it to send a SQL query. Both components exist in their own containers and make network requests as they would normally, unaware that the other container exists on the same server and that the network that connects them is virtual and has been created and managed by Docker.

Once you have tested that the MVC application works, type Control+C to stop monitoring the output and leave the container running in the background. You can check that the container is still running with the docker ps command.

Working with Software-Defined Networks

The virtual network that allowed the containers to communicate in the previous section is an example of a *software-defined network* (SDN). As the name suggests, SDNs are networks that are created and managed using software. SDNs behave like traditional networks and use regular IP addresses ports, but there are no physical network interfaces, and the infrastructure for the networks, such as name services and routing, are provided by Docker.

SDNs allow containers to communicate. Simple SDNs are restricted to a single server. The default network that I used in the previous section, known as the *default bridge network*, is a good example. This network is one of a set that Docker creates when it starts. Run the command shown in Listing 5-30 to see the default networks that Docker provides.

Listing 5-30. Listing the Docker Networks

```
docker network ls
```

This command lists all the current SDNs and produces the following output:

```
NETWORK ID          NAME                DRIVER              SCOPE
3826803e0a8c        bridge              bridge              local
0e643a56cce6        host                host                local
9058e96d6113        none                null                local
```

The host network is the host server's network, and the none network is a network that has no connectivity and that can be used to isolate containers completely. The network whose name is bridge is the one that is of most interest because Docker adds all containers to this network when it creates them. Run the command shown in Listing 5-31 to inspect the default bridge network.

Listing 5-31. Inspecting the Default Bridge Network

```
docker network inspect bridge
```

Now that there are two containers running, you will see an additional entry in the Containers section, showing the network configuration that Docker has applied to the MVC container, like this (although you may see different addresses):

```
...
"Containers": {
    "1be5d5609e232335d539b29c49192c51333aaea1fd822249342827456aefc02e": {
        "Name": "productapp",
        "EndpointID": "3ff7acdaf3cce9e77cfc7156a04d6fa7bf4b5ced3fd13",
        "MacAddress": "02:42:ac:11:00:03",
        "IPv4Address": "172.17.0.3/16",
        "IPv6Address": ""
    },
    "9dd1568078b63104abc145840df8502ec2e171f94157596236f00458ffbf0f02": {
        "Name": "mysql",
        "EndpointID": "72b3df290f3fb955e1923b04909b7f27fa3854d8df583",
        "MacAddress": "02:42:ac:11:00:02",
        "IPv4Address": "172.17.0.2/16",
        "IPv6Address": ""
    }
},
...
```

The best way to understand the effect of the Docker SDN is to understand the composition of the application that was created in the previous section and to consider the connectivity of the MVC and MySQL containers, as illustrated in Figure 5-2.

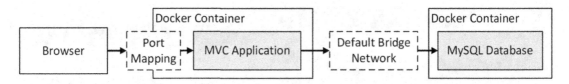

Figure 5-2. *Using the default bridge network*

The browser sends its HTTP request to a port on the host operating system that Docker maps to a port in the MVC application's container. The MVC application asks Entity Framework Core to provide it with data, which it does by using the default bridge network to communicate with the MySQL application running in a separate container. The command in Listing 5-16 that created the MySQL container didn't include a port mapping, which means that the MySQL container isn't accessible via a port on the host operating system.

■ **Note**   The software-defined networks created in this chapter exist only on a single host server, which means that all the containers connected to the network must be running on that server. Docker also supports software-defined networks that span all the nodes in a cluster of servers, which I demonstrate in Chapter 7.

Scaling the MVC Application

Software-defined networks behave like physical networks, and containers behave like servers connected to them. This means that scaling up the MVC application so that there are multiple ASP.NET Core servers is as simple as creating and starting additional containers. Run the command in Listing 5-32 to add a new MVC container. (Enter the command as a single line.)

Listing 5-32. Creating an Additional MVC Application Container

```
docker run -d --name productapp2 -p 3500:80 -e DBHOST=172.17.0.2
    -e MESSAGE="2nd Server" apress/exampleapp
```

When creating additional containers for an application, it is important to ensure the new containers have different names (productapp2 in this case) and different port mappings (port 3500, instead of port 3000, is mapped to port 80 for this container). To further differentiate the new container, the -e argument has been used to set the MESSAGE environment variable, which will be displayed in the MVC application's output. The -d argument tells Docker to start the container in the background.

The result is that there are containers for the MVC application that will handle requests on ports 3000 and 3500 of the host server. To test the containers, open browser tabs and request http://localhost:3000 and http://localhost:3500, which will produce the results shown in Figure 5-3. Notice that the banner in the response from the new container says "2nd Server," differentiating it from the original container.

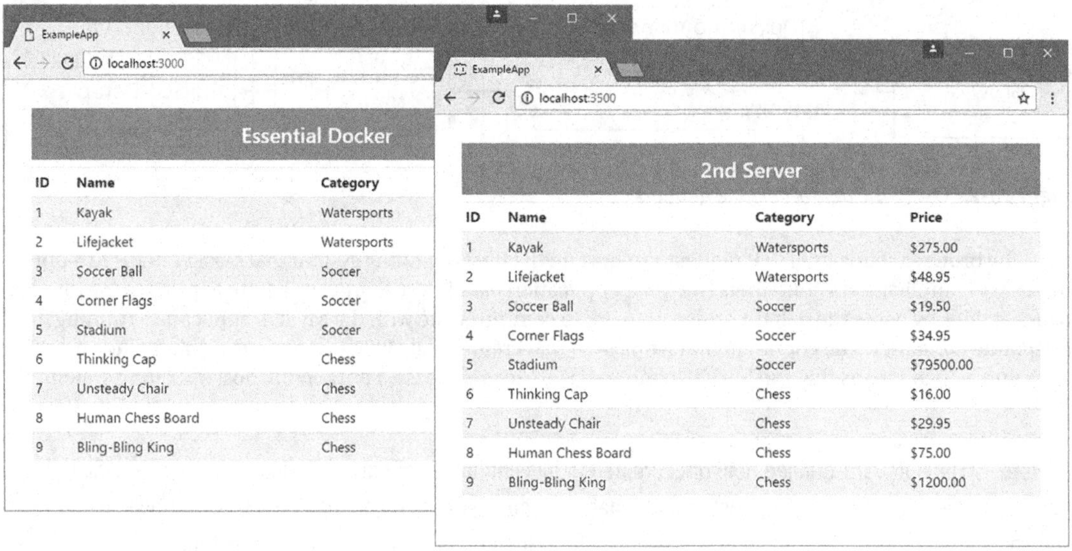

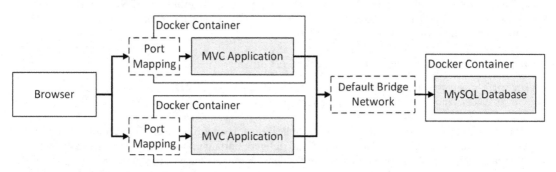

Figure 5-3. *Creating additional application containers*

Figure 5-4 shows the composition of the application following the addition of a second MVC application container.

Figure 5-4. *The effect of adding an additional container*

Docker assigns each container its own IP address, and the containers can communicate freely with one another.

Creating Custom Software-Defined Networks

Using the default bridge network demonstrates the basic networking features of Docker, but it has two main limitations. The first limitation is the awkward process of inspecting the network to get the IP address of the MySQL container to configure the MVC containers.

The second limitation is that all the containers are connected to the same network, while large-scale applications are generally designed with multiple networks that separate out the different functional areas so they can be monitored and managed independently. Fortunately, both of these limitations can be addressed by creating custom SDNs instead of using the default bridge network.

To prepare for this section, run the command shown in Listing 5-33 to stop and remove the database and MVC containers.

Listing 5-33. Removing the Containers

```
docker rm -f $(docker ps -aq)
```

Creating Custom Networks

Custom software-defined networks are created using the `docker network create` command, followed by the name for the new network. Run the commands shown in Listing 5-34 to create two new software-defined networks called `frontend` and `backend`.

Listing 5-34. Creating Custom Software-Defined Networks

```
docker network create frontend
docker network create backend
```

The `frontend` network will be used to receive HTTP requests by the MVC containers. The backend network will be used for SQL queries between the MVC containers and the MySQL container. Run the `docker network ls` command and you will see that the output includes the new networks, like this:

```
NETWORK ID      NAME        DRIVER      SCOPE
778d9eb6777a    backend     bridge      local
fa1bc701b306    bridge      bridge      local
2f0bb28d5716    frontend    bridge      local
0e643a56cce6    host        host        local
9058e96d6113    none        null        local
```

Connecting Containers to Custom Networks

Once you have created custom networks, you can connect containers to them using the `--network` argument, which can be used with the `docker create` and `docker run` commands. Run the command shown in Listing 5-35 to create a new database container that is connected to the backend network. (Enter the command as a single line.)

Listing 5-35. Creating a Container Connected to a Network

```
docker run -d --name mysql -v productdata:/var/lib/mysql --network=backend
    -e MYSQL_ROOT_PASSWORD=mysecret -e bind-address=0.0.0.0 mysql:8.0.0
```

There is one new argument in this command, which is described in Table 5-4.

Table 5-4. *Additional Argument Used to Create the MySQL Container*

Name	Description
`--network`	This argument is used to assign a container to a network. In this case, the container is assigned to the network called backend.

Notice that there are no port mappings in this command, which means the database cannot be reached through the host operating system. Instead, it will only be able to receive connections through the backend software-defined network.

Understanding the Docker DNS Service

Docker configures containers so their Domain Name System (DNS) requests resolve the names assigned to containers to the IP addresses they have been given on custom software-defined networks. (This feature is not available on the default bridge network.)

The DNS configuration means that container names can be used as host names, avoiding the need to locate the IP address assigned to a container. Run the command shown in Listing 5-36 to perform a simple test of the Docker DNS feature.

Listing 5-36. Testing the Docker DNS Feature

```
docker run -it --rm --network backend alpine:3.4 ping -c 3 mysql
```

This command creates and runs an image using the Alpine Linux distribution and executes the ping command to a host called mysql, which Docker will automatically resolve to the IP address that has been assigned to the mysql container on the backend software-defined network. The command will produce the following results:

```
...
PING mysql (172.19.0.2): 56 data bytes
64 bytes from 172.19.0.2: seq=0 ttl=64 time=0.070 ms
64 bytes from 172.19.0.2: seq=1 ttl=64 time=0.124 ms
64 bytes from 172.19.0.2: seq=2 ttl=64 time=0.128 ms

--- mysql ping statistics ---
3 packets transmitted, 3 packets received, 0% packet loss
round-trip min/avg/max = 0.070/0.107/0.128 Microsoft
...
```

Once the ping command is complete, the container will exit and be removed automatically.

Creating the MVC Containers

The embedded DNS feature and the fact that port mappings are not required makes it simpler to create multiple MVC application containers because only the container names must be unique. Run the commands shown in Listing 5-37 to create three containers for the MVC application. Each command should be entered on a single line.

Listing 5-37. Creating the MVC Application Containers

```
docker create --name productapp1 -e DBHOST=mysql -e MESSAGE="1st Server"
    --network backend apress/exampleapp
docker create --name productapp2 -e DBHOST=mysql -e MESSAGE="2nd Server"
    --network backend apress/exampleapp
docker create --name productapp3 -e DBHOST=mysql -e MESSAGE="3rd Server"
    --network backend apress/exampleapp
```

The docker run and docker create commands can connect a container only to a single network. The commands in Listing 5-37 specified the backend network, but this is only one of the connections needed for the MVC containers. Run the commands in Listing 5-38 to connect the MVC containers to the frontend network as well.

Listing 5-38. Connecting the Application Containers to Another Network

```
docker network connect frontend productapp1
docker network connect frontend productapp2
docker network connect frontend productapp3
```

The docker network connect command connects existing containers to software-defined networks. The commands in the listing connect the three MVC containers to the frontend network.

Now that the MVC application containers have been connected to both Docker networks, run the command in Listing 5-39 to start them.

Listing 5-39. Starting the Application Containers

```
docker start productapp1 productapp2 productapp3
```

Adding a Load Balancer

The MVC containers were created without port mappings, which means they are accessible only through the Docker software-defined networks and cannot be reached through the host operating system.

The missing piece of the puzzle is a load balancer, which will receive HTTP requests on a single port mapped to the host operating system and distribute them to the MVC application containers over the frontend Docker network.

There are lots of options when it comes to load balancers, and the choice is usually tied to the infrastructure platform to which the application is deployed. For example, if you are deploying your application into a corporate network, you are likely to find that there are load balancers already installed and running. Equally, most cloud platforms will offer a load balancer service, although its use is often optional.

For this example, I have selected HAProxy, which is an excellent HTTP load balancer that has been adopted by Docker for use in its cloud environment and provided through an image that I use in Chapter 6.

■ **Tip**   HAProxy can be used in a Linux container but doesn't provide support for Windows. If you are using Windows containers and require a load balancer, then consider Nginx (http://nginx.org).

To configure HAProxy, add a file called haproxy.cfg to the ExampleApp folder with the content shown in Listing 5-40.

Listing 5-40. The Contents of the haproxy.cfg File in the ExampleApp Folder

```
defaults
    timeout connect 5000
    timeout client  50000
    timeout server  50000

frontend localnodes
    bind *:80
    mode http
    default_backend mvc
```

```
backend mvc
    mode http
    balance roundrobin
    server mvc1 productapp1:80
    server mvc2 productapp2:80
    server mvc3 productapp3:80
```

This configuration tells HAProxy to receive connections on port 80, which will be exposed through a mapping on the host operating system, and distribute them to the three MVC containers, which are identified using their container names, to take advantage of the Docker DNS feature. HTTP requests will be distributed to each MVC container in turn, which makes it easier to test the load balancer and show that all the MVC containers are being used.

If you are using Visual Studio, you must make sure the character encoding and line endings in the haproxy.cfg file meet the expectations of the HAProxy application. Select File ➤ Save As and click the down arrow on the Save button to select the Save With Encoding option. Select the options shown in Figure 5-5 and save the file. If you don't change the configuration, the HAProxy process won't be able to read its configuration file and will report an error.

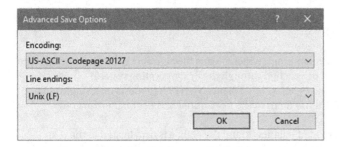

Figure 5-5. *Configuring the save options for the load balancer configuration file*

MATCHING LOAD BALANCING AND SESSION STORAGE STRATEGIES

This configuration uses the HAProxy round-robin load balancing strategy, which sends a request to each of the servers in turn. If your application uses session data, you must ensure that your load balancing strategy suits your session storage model. If each application container maintains its own isolated storage, then you must configure the load balancer so that subsequent requests from a client return to the same server. This can mean that HTTP requests are not evenly distributed but ensures that sessions work as expected. If you store your session data so that it is accessible from any of the application containers, then round-robin load balancing will be fine. See your load balancer configuration settings for the options available. If you are using HAProxy, then the configuration options can be found at www.haproxy.org.

To make the configuration file for the load balancer available, I am going to use a Docker volumes feature that allows files and folders from the host operating system to provide the contents of a directory in a container's file system, rather than requiring a dedicated Docker volume. For Windows and macOS, some configuration is required (no such configuration is required for Linux).

For Windows users, right-click the Docker icon in the task bar and select Settings from the pop-up menu. Click Shared Drives and check the box for the drive that contains the `ExampleApp` folder, as shown in Figure 5-6.

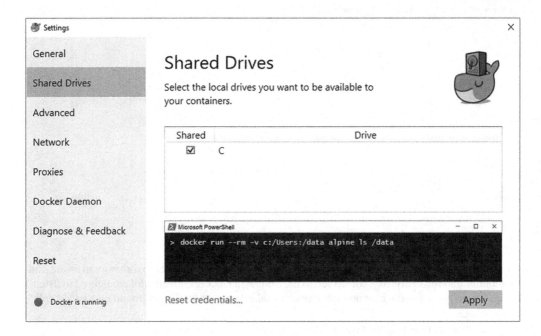

Figure 5-6. *Enabling drive sharing on Windows*

Click Apply, provide the administrator's account password if prompted, and close the Settings window.

For macOS users, click the Docker menu bar icon and select Preference from the pop-up menu. Click File Sharing and ensure that the folder that contains the `ExampleApp` folder is on the list of shared directories, as shown in Figure 5-7.

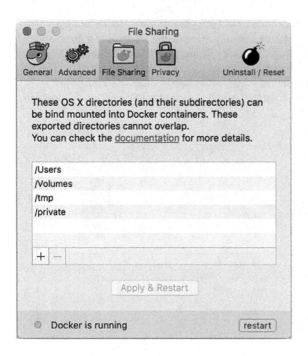

Figure 5-7. *Enabling drive sharing on macOS*

For all operating systems, run the command in Listing 5-41 from the `ExampleApp` directory to create and start new container that runs HAProxy, connected to the front-end Docker network and configured to listen for HTTP requests on port 80 of the host operating system. Take care to enter the command on a single line.

Listing 5-41. Creating and Starting the Load Balancer Container

```
docker run -d --name loadbalancer --network frontend
    -v "$(pwd)/haproxy.cfg:/usr/local/etc/haproxy/haproxy.cfg"
    -p 3000:80 haproxy:1.7.0
```

Enter the command on a single line. The `-v` argument in this command tells Docker to mount the `haproxy.cfg` file that is in the `ExampleApp` folder in the container so that it appears in the `/usr/local/etc/haproxy` directory. This is a useful feature for creating containers that require configuration files. (It is also useful for containerized development environments, which I describe in Chapter 8.)

The `--network` argument connects the load balancer container to the `frontend` network so that it can communicate with the MVC containers. The `-p` argument maps port 3000 on the host operating system to port 80 in the container so that the load balancer can receive requests from the outside world.

■ **Tip**   If you see an error when the container starts, then you most likely forgot to change the character encoding for the `haproxy.cfg` file, as shown in Figure 5-4. Change the settings, save the configuration file, and then run `docker rm -f loadbalancer` to remove the container before repeating the command in Listing 5-41.

Once the load balancer has started, open a browser tab and request the URL `http://localhost:3000`. Reload the page and you will see that the load balancer distributes the request between the MVC application containers, which is reflected in the banner shown in the response, as illustrated by Figure 5-8. (The first request to each MVC container may take a second as the application starts up, but if you keep reloading, subsequent requests should be handled immediately.)

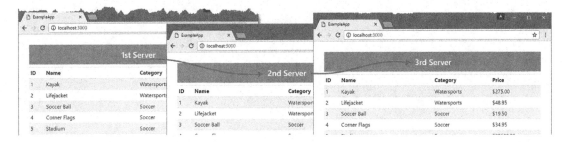

Figure 5-8. *Load balancing between multiple application containers*

The final result is an application that contains five containers, two software-defined networks, and a single port mapping. The composition of the application is shown in Figure 5-9 and is similar to the way that applications are conventionally composed, albeit all the components are running on a single host server and are isolated by containers.

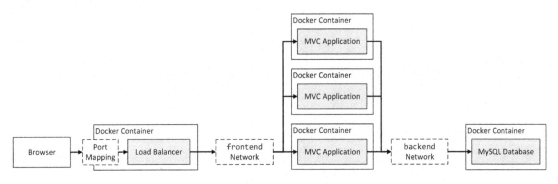

Figure 5-9. *The composition of an application with multiple software-defined networks*

The database container is connected only to the backend network. The MVC application containers are connected to both the frontend and backend networks; they receive HTTP requests through the frontend network and make SQL queries over the backend network. The load balancer container is connected only to the frontend network and has a port mapping onto the host operating system; it receives HTTP requests via the port mapping and distributes them to the MVC application containers.

Summary

In this chapter, I described the Docker volume and software-defined networking features, which allow more complex applications to be composed by combining containers. I explained how volumes are used to keep data files outside of a container's storage and how this changes the way that Entity Framework Core is used to create database schemas. I also introduced software-defined networks and showed you how they can be used to create a familiar structure for an application, even though all the components exist in Docker containers rather than on dedicated server hardware. In the next chapter, I show you how to describe more complex applications without having to create and manage the containers, volumes, and networks individually.

CHAPTER 6

■ ■ ■

Docker Compose

In the previous chapter, I showed you how a complex application can be created by combining containers, volumes, and software-defined networks. The problem with this approach is that each step has to be performed manually, which can be an error-prone process. Not only does each command have to be entered correctly, but the steps have to be performed in the order covered in Chapter 5 because the container relies on being able to send network requests to the container created before it. If you skip a step or perform a step out of order, then you may not end up with a working application.

In this chapter, I show you how to use *Docker Compose*, which is used to describe complex applications in a consistent and predictable manner. A *compose file* contains details of all the volumes, networks, and containers that make up an application and the relationships between them. I explain how Docker Compose is used and demonstrate how to describe the example application using a compose file so that all the components it needs can be created and started in a single step. Table 6-1 puts Docker Compose into context.

Table 6-1. *Putting Docker Compose in Context*

Question	Answer
What is it?	Docker Compose is a tool that is used to describe complex applications and manage the containers, networks, and volumes they require.
Why is it useful?	Docker Compose simplifies the process of setting up and running applications so that you don't have to type in complex commands, which can lead to configuration errors.
How is it used?	The description of the application and its requirements is defined in a compose file, which is processed using the `docker-compose` command. The number of containers in an application is changed using the `docker-compose scale` command.
Are there any pitfalls or limitations?	Docker doesn't provide any way to wait for the application in one container to be ready to receive requests from another container. As a consequence, you must manage the dependencies between the containers in an application directly.
Are there any alternatives?	You do not have to use Docker Compose. You can create and manage your containers manually or use an alternative such as Crowdr (`https://github.com/polonskiy/crowdr`).

© Adam Freeman 2017
A. Freeman, *Essential Docker for ASP.NET Core MVC*, DOI 10.1007/978-1-4842-2778-7_6

Table 6-2 summarizes the chapter.

Table 6-2. *Chapter Summary*

Problem	Solution	Listing
Describe a complex application	Use a Docker Compose file	1–5, 7, 17, 18
Process the contents of a compose file	Use the docker-compose build command	6, 8, 20
Create and start the components in a compose file	Use the docker-compose up command	9, 21, 22
Remove the components in a compose file	Use the docker-compose down command	10, 27
Wait until an application is ready to receive connections	Use the wait-for-it package (for Linux containers) or create a PowerShell script (for Windows containers)	11–16, 19
Change the number of containers running for a service	Use the docker-compose scale command	23, 25
List the running services	Use the docker-compose ps command	24
Stop the containers that have been started using a compose file	Use the docker-compose stop command	26

Preparing for This Chapter

This chapter depends on the ExampleApp MVC project created in Chapter 3 and modified in the chapters since. If you don't want to work through the process of creating the example, you can get the project as part of the free source code download that accompanies this book. See the apress.com page for this book.

To ensure that there is no conflict with examples from previous chapters, run the commands shown in Listing 6-1 to remove the containers, networks, and volumes that were created in the previous chapter. Ignore any errors or warnings these commands produce.

Listing 6-1. Removing the Containers, Networks, and Volumes

```
docker rm -f $(docker ps -aq)
docker network rm $(docker network ls -q)
docker volume rm $(docker volume ls -q)
```

Changing the View Message

In this chapter, I demonstrate how to scale up an MVC application by creating multiple containers automatically. To help show which container is handling a specific HTTP request, Listing 6-2 shows a change to the Home controller, altering the message passed by the action method to its view.

Listing 6-2. Changing the Banner in the HomeController.cs File in the ExampleApp/Controllers Folder

```
using Microsoft.AspNetCore.Mvc;
using ExampleApp.Models;
using Microsoft.Extensions.Configuration;
```

```
namespace ExampleApp.Controllers {
    public class HomeController : Controller {
        private IRepository repository;
        private string message;

        public HomeController(IRepository repo, IConfiguration config) {
            repository = repo;
            message = $"Essential Docker ({config["HOSTNAME"]})";
        }

        public IActionResult Index() {
            ViewBag.Message = message;
            return View(repository.Products);
        }
    }
}
```

Docker creates a HOSTNAME environment variable inside containers, which is set to the unique ID of the container. The change to the controller ensures that the response from the application indicates which container handles the request. This is not something you should do in real projects, but it is a useful way to demonstrate how key Docker Compose features work.

Installing Docker Compose on Linux

Docker Compose is included in the Docker installers for Windows and macOS but must be installed separately in Linux. If you are a Linux user, run the commands shown in Listing 6-3 to download and install Docker Compose.

Listing 6-3. Installing Docker Compose for Linux

```
sudo curl -L "https://github.com/docker/compose/releases/download/1.11.2/docker-compose-
$(uname -s)-$(uname -m)" -o /usr/local/bin/docker-compose
sudo chmod +x /usr/local/bin/docker-compose
```

Once the installation is complete, run command shown in Listing 6-4 to check that Docker Compose works as expected.

Listing 6-4. Checking Docker Compose

```
docker-compose --version
```

If the installation has been successful, you will see this response: docker-compose version 1.11.2, build dfed245.

Creating the Compose File

Docker Compose allows complex applications to be described in a configuration file, known as a compose file, that ensures that all the components are set up correctly when the application is deployed.

The starting point is to create the compose. Create a file called docker-compose.yml, which is the conventional name for the compose file, in the ExampleApp folder and add the configuration statements shown in Listing 6-5.

Listing 6-5. The Contents of the docker-compose.yml File in the ExampleApp Folder

```
version: "3"

volumes:
  productdata:

networks:
  frontend:
  backend:
```

The yml file extension denotes that the compose file is expressed in the YAML format, which is introduced in the "*Getting Started with YAML*" sidebar. Table 6-3 describes the configuration properties in Listing 6-5.

Table 6-3. *The Initial Docker Compose Configuration Properties*

Name	Description
version	This setting specifies the version of the Docker Compose schema that the file uses. At the time of writing, the latest version is 3.
volumes	This setting is used to configure the volumes that will be used by the containers defined in the compose file. This example defines a volume called productdata.
networks	This setting is used to configure the software-defined networks that will be used by the containers defined in the compose file. This example defines networks called frontend and backend.

The version section tells Docker which version of the compose file schema is being used. As I write this, the latest version is 3, which includes support for the latest Docker features. Docker is a rapidly evolving platform, so you may find that there is a later version available by the time you read this, although the examples in this chapter should still work as long as you don't change the version setting in the compose file.

GETTING STARTED WITH YAML

YAML is a format used to create configuration files that are human-readable, although it can be confusing when you first start using it. Editing YAML is a lot simpler with the extensions for Visual Studio and Visual Studio Code described in Chapter 3.

The most important aspect of YAML to bear in mind is that indentation with spaces is used to signify the structure of the file and that tabs are forbidden. This runs counter to most file formats that programmers use, where indentation can be adjusted or ignored and tabs can be used freely. In Listing 6-5, for example, the version and networks keywords must have no indentation because they are top-level configuration sections, and the frontend and backend entries are indented by two spaces to indicate they are part of the networks section.

The simplest way to avoid problems with YAML for the examples in this chapter is to use the file from the source code download linked from the apress.com page for this book. But as you start using YAML in your own projects, there are three sources of information that will provide you with the details you require to create compose files.

The first source is the Docker compose file reference, https://docs.docker.com/compose/compose-file, which describes each entry that a compose file contains and provides useful YAML examples.

The second source of information is the schema for the compose file, https://github.com/docker/compose/blob/master/compose/config/config_schema_v3.0.json, which explains how an entry is expressed in YAML. YAML represents data using three primitive structures: key/value maps or objects, lists, and scalars (which are strings or numbers). The compose file schema tells you which of the primitives is used and provides details of any additional requirements.

The final source of information is the YAML standard, http://yaml.org/spec/1.2/spec.html, which will help you make sense of the YAML structure. You won't often need to refer to the standard, but it can throw some light on what is important in a YAML document, which can be helpful when Docker Compose reports errors parsing your files.

Compose files are processed using a command-line tool called docker-compose (note the hyphen), which builds and manages the application.

There is little useful configuration in the example compose file at the moment, but run the command shown in Listing 6-6 in the ExampleApp folder to build the application anyway, just to make sure everything is working.

Listing 6-6. Building the Application

```
docker-compose -f docker-compose.yml build
```

The -f argument is used to specify the name of the compose file, although Docker will default to using docker-compose.yml or docker-compose.yaml if a file isn't specified. The build argument tells Docker to process the file and build the Docker images it contains. There are no images defined in the file at the moment, so you will see the following output:

```
...
WARNING: Some networks were defined but are not used by any service: frontend, backend
...
```

This warning indicates that the compose file tells Docker to create some software-defined networks, but they are not used anywhere else in the application and so they were not created.

If you see an error, go back and check that you have used tabs to re-create the structure as shown in Listing 6-5 and that you have remembered to add a colon after the networks, frontend, and backend configuration entries.

Composing the Database

The process for describing the application using Docker Compose follows the same path as creating the containers manually, and the next step is to configure the database container. Listing 6-7 shows the additions to the compose file that sets up the container for MySQL.

Listing 6-7. Defining the Database Container in the docker-compose.yml File in the ExampleApp Folder

```
version: "3"

volumes:
  productdata:

networks:
  frontend:
  backend:

services:

  mysql:
    image: "mysql:8.0.0"
    volumes:
      - productdata:/var/lib/mysql
    networks:
      - backend
    environment:
      - MYSQL_ROOT_PASSWORD=mysecret
      - bind-address=0.0.0.0
```

The services keyword is used to denote the section of the compose file that contains the descriptions that will be used to create containers. The term *service* is used because the description can be used to create more than one container. Each service is given its own section, as you will see as the compose file is expanded throughout the rest of the chapter.

The service described in Listing 6-7 is called mysql, and it describes how database containers should be created using the configuration properties described in Table 6-4.

Table 6-4. *The Configuration Properties for the MySQL Service*

Name	Description
services	This property denotes the start of the services section of the compose file, which describes the services that will be used to create containers.
mysql	This property denotes the start of a service description called mysql.
image	This property specifies the Docker image that will be used to create containers. In this example, the official MySQL image will be used.
volumes	This property specifies the volumes that will be used by containers and the directories they will be used for. In this example, the productdata volume will be used to provide the contents of the /var/lib/mysql directory.
networks	This property specifies the networks that containers will be connected to. In this example, containers will be connected to the backend network. (The networks keyword used in a service has a different meaning than the top-level network keyword described in Table 6-3.)
environment	This property is used to define the environment variables that will be used when a container is created. In this example, MYSQL_ROOT_PASSWORD and bind-address variables are defined.

Run the command shown in Listing 6-8 in the `ExampleApp` folder to check that the changes you have made to the file can be processed.

Listing 6-8. Building the Application

```
docker-compose build
```

I am able to omit the name of the file because I am using the compose file name that Docker looks for by default. This command will produce output like this:

```
...
WARNING: Some networks were defined but are not used by any service: frontend
mysql uses an image, skipping
...
```

The warning about the unused networks has changed because the database container will be connected to the backend network. The other part of the output indicates that no action is needed for the `mysql` service at the moment because it is based on an existing image, which will be used to create and configure a container when the compose file is used to start the application.

Testing the Application Setup and Teardown

There is just enough configuration in the compose file to run a simple test. Run the command shown in Listing 6-9 in the `ExampleApp` folder to tell Docker Compose to process the compose file and start the application.

Listing 6-9. Running the Composed Application

```
docker-compose up
```

The `docker-compose up` command tells Docker to process the contents of the compose file and set up the volumes, networks, and containers that it specifies. Docker will pull any images that are required from the Docker Hub so they can be used to create a container.

Details of the setup process are shown in the command prompt, along with the output from the containers that are created. There is only one container at the moment, but others are added in the sections that follow. The first part of the output shows the configuration process that Docker Compose goes through.

```
...
WARNING: Some networks were defined but are not used by any service: frontend
Creating network "exampleapp_backend" with the default driver
Creating volume "exampleapp_productdata" with default driver
Creating exampleapp_mysql_1
Attaching to exampleapp_mysql_1
...
```

The name of the network, the volume, and the container that Docker creates are prefixed with `example_`. The network is called `exampleapp_backend`, the volume is called `exampleapp_productdata`, and the container is called `example_mysql_1`. (The `_1` part of the MySQL container name refers to how Docker scales up applications described using compose files, which I describe in the *"Scaling the MVC Service"* section.)

The prefix is taken from the name of the directory that contains the compose file, and it ensures that different compose files can use the same names for networks, volumes, and containers without them conflicting when the application is started. (You can change the prefix used with the -p argument for the docker-compose up command, which I demonstrate in Chapter 8.)

Once the database has finished its initialization process, type Control+C to terminate the docker-compose command and stop the containers described in the compose file.

You can explore the effect of the compose file using the standard Docker commands. Run the docker ps -a command to see the containers that have been created. Run the docker network ls command to see the software-defined network (only one of the two networks specified in the compose file has been created because no container currently connects to the front_end network). Run the docker volume ls command to see the volumes that have been created.

Run the command shown in Listing 6-10 in the ExampleApp folder to remove the containers and networks that are described in the compose file (but not the volume, which persists unless you use the -v argument).

Listing 6-10. Removing the Networks and Containers

```
docker-compose down
```

Database Preparation and MVC Composition

In the previous chapter, I relied on the ASP.NET Core MVC application to ensure that the schema in the MySQL database was up-to-date by automatically applying the Entity Framework Core migrations during startup.

This approach is fine in development and for simple projects, but automatically applying database migrations can lead to data loss in production systems and should be done with caution. Entity Framework Core migrations are groups of SQL commands that alter the database schema to reflect changes in the MVC application's data model classes. If you remove a property from a model class, for example, the migration that reflects that change will drop a corresponding column from a table in the database. Automating any process that affects a production database is risky. I recommend you apply database migrations explicitly only as part of a controlled upgrade and not implicitly as part of the regular application startup.

That doesn't mean that database migrations have to be hand-typed into the command prompt as part of an upgrade. The approach that I take in this chapter uses the same ASP.NET Core project to create two different containers. One container will perform the database initialization and apply the Entity Framework Core migrations, while the other will run the ASP.NET Core MVC application.

Modifying the MVC Application

Rather than create a new .NET project to initialize the database, I am going to reconfigure the existing application so that it has two modes: database initialization and normal ASP.NET Core MVC service.

Modify the database context class, as shown in Listing 6-11, so that it can be instantiated using a parameterless constructor, allowing it to be used outside of the ASP.NET Core startup sequence.

Listing 6-11. Preparing for Initialization in the ProductDbContext.cs File in the ExampleApp/Models Folder

```
using Microsoft.EntityFrameworkCore;
using System;

namespace ExampleApp.Models {

    public class ProductDbContext : DbContext {

        public ProductDbContext() { }
```

```
public ProductDbContext(DbContextOptions<ProductDbContext> options)
    : base(options) {
}

protected override void OnConfiguring(DbContextOptionsBuilder options) {

    var envs = Environment.GetEnvironmentVariables();

    var host = envs["DBHOST"] ?? "localhost";
    var port = envs["DBPORT"] ?? "3306";
    var password = envs["DBPASSWORD"] ?? "mysecret";

    options.UseMySql($"server={host};userid=root;pwd={password};"
            + $"port={port};database=products");
}

    public DbSet<Product> Products { get; set; }
    }
}
```

The OnConfiguring method will be called when a new database context is created and provides Entity Framework Core with the connection string that it needs to connect to the database. The configuration for the connection string is obtained from the application's environment variables, accessed through the System.Envionment class.

Make the changes shown in Listing 6-12 to the Program class, which is responsible for the startup of the application.

Listing 6-12. Preparing for Database Initialization in the Program.cs File in the ExampleApp Folder

```
using System;
using System.Collections.Generic;
using System.IO;
using System.Linq;
using System.Threading.Tasks;
using Microsoft.AspNetCore.Hosting;
using Microsoft.Extensions.Configuration;

namespace ExampleApp {
    public class Program {
        public static void Main(string[] args) {
            var config = new ConfigurationBuilder()
                .AddCommandLine(args)
              .AddEnvironmentVariables()
                .Build();

            if ((config["INITDB"] ?? "false") == "true") {
                System.Console.WriteLine("Preparing Database...");
                Models.SeedData.EnsurePopulated(new Models.ProductDbContext());
                System.Console.WriteLine("Database Preparation Complete");
            } else {
                System.Console.WriteLine("Starting ASP.NET...");
                var host = new WebHostBuilder()
```

```
                .UseConfiguration(config)
                .UseKestrel()
                .UseContentRoot(Directory.GetCurrentDirectory())
                .UseIISIntegration()
                .UseStartup<Startup>()
                .Build();

            host.Run();
        }
    }
  }
}
```

If the configuration setting called INITDB is set to true, then the database will be initialized when the .NET runtime invokes the Main method. If the configuration setting is not true or is not defined, then the ASP.NET Core MVC application will be started instead. The value for the INITDB setting will be read from the command line and from the environment variables, which will allow the database to be easily upgraded from a command prompt and within a container.

Reading configuration data from the command line requires the addition of a NuGet package. Edit the ExampleApp.csproj file to make the addition shown in Listing 6-13.

Listing 6-13. Adding a Package in the ExampleApp.csproj File in the ExampleApp Folder

```
<Project Sdk="Microsoft.NET.Sdk.Web">

  <PropertyGroup>
    <TargetFramework>netcoreapp1.1</TargetFramework>
  </PropertyGroup>

  <ItemGroup>
    <PackageReference Include="Microsoft.AspNetCore" Version="1.1.1" />
    <PackageReference Include="Microsoft.AspNetCore.Mvc" Version="1.1.2" />
    <PackageReference Include="Microsoft.AspNetCore.StaticFiles" Version="1.1.1" />
    <PackageReference Include="Microsoft.Extensions.Logging.Debug" Version="1.1.1" />
    <PackageReference Include="Microsoft.VisualStudio.Web.BrowserLink" Version="1.1.0" />
    <PackageReference Include="Microsoft.EntityFrameworkCore" Version="1.1.1" />
    <PackageReference Include="Microsoft.EntityFrameworkCore.Tools" Version="1.1.0" />
    <PackageReference Include="Pomelo.EntityFrameworkCore.MySql" Version="1.1.0" />
    <DotNetCliToolReference Include="Microsoft.EntityFrameworkCore.Tools.DotNet"
    Version="1.0.0" />
    <PackageReference Include="Microsoft.Extensions.Configuration.CommandLine"
    Version="1.1.1" />
  </ItemGroup>
</Project>
```

Finally, comment out the statement in the Startup class that was previously responsible for initializing the database, as shown in Listing 6-14.

Listing 6-14. Disabling the Initialization Call in the Startup.cs File in the ExampleApp Folder

```
...
public void Configure(IApplicationBuilder app,
    IHostingEnvironment env, ILoggerFactory loggerFactory) {

    loggerFactory.AddConsole();
    loggerFactory.AddDebug();
    app.UseDeveloperExceptionPage();
    app.UseStatusCodePages();
    app.UseStaticFiles();
    app.UseMvcWithDefaultRoute();

    //SeedData.EnsurePopulated(app);
}
...
```

Describing the Database Initialization and MVC Services

When the application was set up step by step in Chapter 5, each component was allowed to go through its startup routine before the components that depended on it were started. This meant, for example, that MySQL was given the time to go through its lengthy first-start procedure before the MVC application was started, ensuring that the MySQL database was ready to start receiving SQL queries before the MVC application started making them.

Docker doesn't support this gradual model of initializing an application when a compose file is used. Docker has no insight into whether MySQL is ready to accept network connections and just starts one container after another, with the potential outcome that the MVC application will fail because it tries to make a request to a database that isn't ready.

To ensure that queries are not sent until the database is ready, I am going to use a package called wait-for-it, which waits until a TCP port is accepting connections. Run the command shown in Listing 6-15 in the ExampleApp folder to download the wait-for-it package using NPM so that it is installed in a folder called a folder called node_modules.

Listing 6-15. Downloading the wait-for-it Package

```
npm install wait-for-it.sh@1.0.0
```

Once the download is complete, apply the changes shown in Listing 6-16 to update the Docker file for the MVC application. These changes use the wait-for-it package to defer the startup of the .NET Core application until the database is ready to receive connections.

Listing 6-16. Waiting for the Database in the Dockerfile File in the ExampleApp Folder

```
FROM microsoft/aspnetcore:1.1.1

COPY dist /app

COPY node_modules/wait-for-it.sh/bin/wait-for-it /app/wait-for-it.sh

RUN chmod +x /app/wait-for-it.sh

WORKDIR /app

EXPOSE 80/tcp
```

```
ENV WAITHOST=mysql WAITPORT=3306

ENTRYPOINT ./wait-for-it.sh $WAITHOST:$WAITPORT --timeout=0 \
    && exec dotnet ExampleApp.dll
```

The host name and TCP port that will be checked by the wait-for-it package are specified using environment variables called WAITHOST and WAITPORT. Listing 6-17 adds services to the compose file that uses the new application configuration and the waiting feature to prepare the database and run the MVC application.

Listing 6-17. Describing the Database Initialization and MVC Application in the docker-compose.yml File

```
version: "3"

volumes:
  productdata:

networks:
  frontend:
  backend:

services:

  mysql:
    image: "mysql:8.0.0"
    volumes:
      - productdata:/var/lib/mysql
    networks:
      - backend
    environment:
      - MYSQL_ROOT_PASSWORD=mysecret
      - bind-address=0.0.0.0

  dbinit:
    build:
      context: .
      dockerfile: Dockerfile
    networks:
      - backend
    environment:
      - INITDB=true
      - DBHOST=mysql
    depends_on:
      - mysql

  mvc:
    build:
      context: .
      dockerfile: Dockerfile
    networks:
      - backend
      - frontend
```

```
environment:
  - DBHOST=mysql
depends_on:
  - mysql
```

The new services are called dbinit and mvc. I have taken a different approach for these services, providing Docker with the information it needs to build the images for the services, rather than specifying an image that it can pull from a repository, which is what I did for MySQL. Table 6-5 describes the configuration options used for these services.

Table 6-5. *The Configuration Properties for the Database Initialization and MVC Services*

Name	Description
build	This property denotes the start of the build section, which tells Docker how to create the image required for this service's containers.
build/context	This property defines the context directory that will be used to create the image. For this example, the content is the current directory, which will be the ExampleApp folder when the image is produced.
build/dockerfile	This property specifies the Docker file that will be used to create the image.
networks	This property specifies the software-defined networks that the containers will be connected to. The database initialization container will be connected to the backend network because it needs to communicate with the database. The MVC application containers will be connected to both networks. (The networks keyword used in a service has a different meaning than the top-level network keyword described in Table 6-3.)
environment	This property specifies the environment variables for the containers. For this example, they are used to select the initialization/MVC modes and to provide the name of the database container, which is used in the Entity Framework Core connection string.
depends_on	This property tells Docker the order in which containers must be created. In this example, the containers for the dbinit and mvc containers will be started after the mysql container.

Don't be misled by the depends_on configuration option, which tells Docker the order in which containers should be started. Docker will start the containers in the specified sequence but still won't wait until the applications they contain are initialized, which is why the wait-for-it package is required.

WAITING IN WINDOWS CONTAINERS

The wait-for-it package can be used only in Linux containers. To achieve a similar effect in Windows containers, create a file called wait.ps1 in the ExampleApp folder with the following content:

```
Write-Host "Waiting for:" $env:WAITHOST $env:WAITPORT
do {
    Start-Sleep 1
} until(Test-NetConnection $env:WAITHOST -Port $env:WAITPORT `
    | Where-Object { $_.TcpTestSucceeded });
Write-Host "End of waiting."
```

This is a simple PowerShell script that waits for a TCP port to become available. Use the ADD command to include the script in a Docker file so that it can be used with the ENTRYPOINT command, like this:

```
FROM microsoft/dotnet:1.1.1-runtime-nanoserver

COPY dist /app

COPY wait.ps1 /app/wait.ps1

WORKDIR /app

EXPOSE 80/tcp

ENV ASPNETCORE_URLS http://+:80

ENV WAITHOST=mysql WAITPORT=3306

ENTRYPOINT powershell ./wait.ps1; dotnet ExampleApp.dll
```

The result is the same as using the wait-for-it package, although you may see some warnings displayed in the container output telling you that PowerShell modules cannot be found. These warnings can be ignored.

Composing the Load Balancer

The final service required in the application is the load balancer. I am going to use HAProxy again, which is the package that was used in Chapter 5, but using an image that is published by Docker. Listing 6-18 shows the changes to the docker-compose.yml file to describe the load balancer.

Listing 6-18. Describing the Load Balancer in the docker-compose.yml File in the ExampleApp Folder

```
version: "3"

volumes:
  productdata:

networks:
  frontend:
  backend:

services:

  mysql:
    image: "mysql:8.0.0"
```

```
    volumes:
      - productdata:/var/lib/mysql
    networks:
      - backend
    environment:
      - MYSQL_ROOT_PASSWORD=mysecret
      - bind-address=0.0.0.0

  dbinit:
    build:
      context: .
      dockerfile: Dockerfile
    networks:
      - backend
    environment:
      - INITDB=true
      - DBHOST=mysql
    depends_on:
      - mysql

  mvc:
    build:
      context: .
      dockerfile: Dockerfile
    networks:
      - backend
      - frontend
    environment:
      - DBHOST=mysql
    depends_on:
      - mysql

  loadbalancer:
    image: dockercloud/haproxy:1.2.1
    ports:
      - 3000:80
    links:
      - mvc
    volumes:
      - /var/run/docker.sock:/var/run/docker.sock
    networks:
      - frontend
```

This version of HAProxy is set up to receive events from Docker as containers are created, started, stopped, and destroyed in order to generate configuration files for HAProxy to dynamically reflect changes in the application. Table 6-6 describes the configuration settings that are used to describe the load balancer service.

Table 6-6. *The Configuration Properties for the Load Balancer Service*

Name	Description
image	This property specifies the image that will be used for the load balancer container. In this example, the image is one provided by Docker.
ports	This property specifies the host port mappings that will be applied to the containers. In this example, requests sent to port 3000 on the host operating system will be directed to port 80 inside the container, which is the default port on which HAProxy listens for HTTP requests.
links	This property is used to provide HAProxy with the name of the service whose containers will receive HTTP requests, which is mvc in this example. The load balancer will respond automatically when a new container is created for the mvc service and start forwarding HTTP requests for it to process.
volumes	This property is used to specify the volumes used by the container. In this example, the volumes property is used to allow the load balancer access to the Docker runtime on the host operating system so that it can receive notifications when new containers are created in order to monitor for changes in the service specified by the links property.
networks	This property is used to specify the software-defined networks that the containers will be connected to. In this example, the load balancer will be connected to the frontend network, which will allow it to forward HTTP requests to the MVC application. (The networks keyword used in a service has a different meaning from the top-level network keyword described in Table 6-3.)

Running the Application

The compose file now contains descriptions of all the components required for the example application: a volume for the database files, two software-defined networks, a database container, a container that will prepare the database for its first use, a container for the MVC application, and a load balancer that will receive and distribute HTTP requests. In the sections that follow, I show you how to use these descriptions to run the application.

Processing the Compose File

Run the commands shown in Listing 6-19 in the ExampleApp folder to prepare the .NET Core project, ensuring that the required NuGet packages are installed and that the latest version of the project is published as a self-contained set of files in the dist folder.

Listing 6-19. Preparing the Application for Composition

```
dotnet restore
dotnet publish --framework netcoreapp1.1 --configuration Release --output dist
```

Run the command shown in Listing 6-20 in the ExampleApp folder to process the contents of the compose file.

Listing 6-20. Processing the Compose File

```
docker-compose build
```

When you run the docker-compose build command, Docker will generate new images for the dbinit and mvc services, as described in the compose file and that you can see if you run the docker images command. Docker is smart enough to know that these two services require the same content and generates one image with two tags, which you can see because they have the same ID.

Preparing the Database

Run the command shown in Listing 6-21 in the ExampleApp folder to start and prepare the database.

Listing 6-21. Starting and Preparing the Database

```
docker-compose up dbinit
```

The docker-compose up command can be used to selectively start services. This command specifies the dbinit service, and because of the depends_on setting in the compose file in Listing 6-18, Docker will also start the mysql service. When a service is specified as an argument to the docker-compose up command, only the output from that service is shown, which means you will see output from the database initialization container and not MySQL, like this:

```
...
Creating network "exampleapp_frontend" with the default driver
Creating network "exampleapp_backend" with the default driver
Creating exampleapp_mysql_1
Creating exampleapp_dbinit_1
Attaching to exampleapp_dbinit_1
dbinit_1       | wait-for-it.sh: waiting for mysql:3306 without a timeout
dbinit_1       | wait-for-it.sh: mysql:3306 is available after 10 seconds
dbinit_1       | Preparing Database...
dbinit_1       | Applying Migrations...
dbinit_1       | Created Seed Data...
dbinit_1       | Database Preparation Complete
exampleapp_dbinit_1 exited with code 0
...
```

The wait-for-it script in the dbinit container will wait until the database is ready to accept connections, at which point the Entity Framework Core migration is applied and the seed data is created. The dbinit container will exit once the preparation is complete.

Starting the MVC Application

Now that the database has been prepared, it is time to start the MVC application. Run the command shown in Listing 6-22 in the ExampleApp folder to start the MVC application.

Listing 6-22. Starting the MVC Application

```
docker-compose up mvc loadbalancer
```

This command tells Docker to start the mvc and loadbalancer services. To do that, Docker follows the chain of depends_on settings to determine the other services that must be started. In this case, the mvc service depends on the mysql service, for which there is already a container. Docker will automatically pull any images it requires, create the software-defined networks if they are not already present, and, finally, create and start the containers for each service.

113

Once the new containers have started, open a new browser tab and request the URL http://localhost:3000, which corresponds to the port mapping defined for the load balancer in Listing 6-18. The load balancer will forward the request over the frontend network to the MVC container, which queries the database over the backend network and uses the data it receives to generate the response shown in Figure 6-1. The response from the MVC application includes the ID of its container.

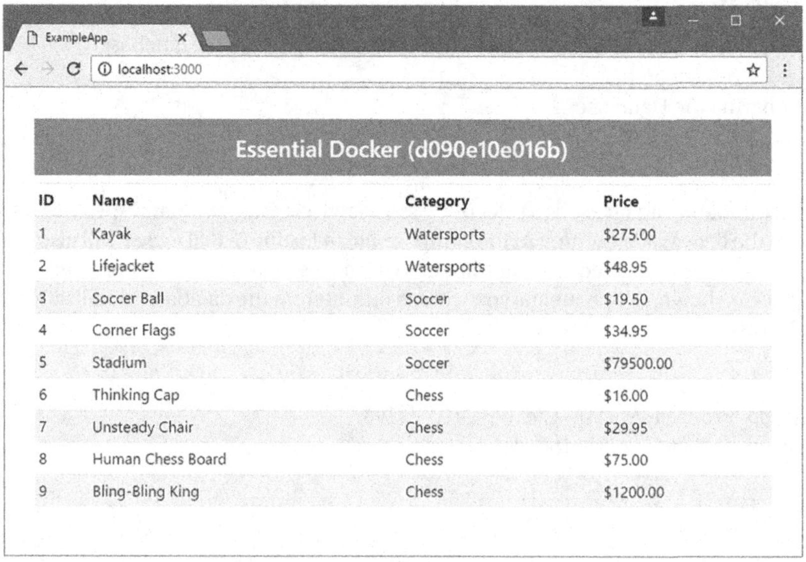

Figure 6-1. *Testing the example application*

Scaling the MVC Service

Compose files describe services for which containers are created. So far, there has been a one-to-one mapping between the descriptions contained in the compose file and the containers that have been created. Docker Compose has an important feature, which is that it will create and manage multiple containers from the same description, meaning that a service can be made up of more than one container, which can share the workload for the application.

When you ran the docker-compose up command in Listing 6-21, Docker created and started three containers: one database container from the mysql service, one MVC container from mvc service, and a load balancer container from the loadbalancer service. It can be hard to see in all of the output from MySQL, but Docker writes messages to the command prompt as it creates each component required for the application, like this:

```
...
exampleapp_mysql_1 is up-to-date
Creating exampleapp_mvc_1
Creating exampleapp_loadbalancer_1
Attaching to exampleapp_mvc_1, exampleapp_loadbalancer_1
...
```

The exampleapp_mysql_1 container was left over from the initialization process, and Docker knows that it doesn't need to be re-created. The exampleapp_mvc_1 and exampleapp_loadbalancer_1 containers had to be created because no containers for those services existed before the docker-compose up command was run. By the time the docker-compose up command completed, there was one container for each of the services specified and for the services named in the depends_on properties.

Docker assigns names to the container with the _1 suffix so that multiple instances of a container can be created without causing a name conflict. Use a second command prompt to run the command shown in Listing 6-23 in the ExampleApp folder.

Listing 6-23. Scaling Up the MVC Application Containers

```
docker-compose scale mvc=4
```

The docker-compose scale command is used to change the number of containers for a service. In this case, the command tells Docker that there should be four instances of the container described by the mvc service in the compose file. The output of the command is the messages that Docker displays as it creates the new containers.

```
...
Creating and starting exampleapp_mvc_2 ... done
Creating and starting exampleapp_mvc_3 ... done
Creating and starting exampleapp_mvc_4 ... done
...
```

You will also see the output from the MVC application displayed in the original command prompt as the containers are started and the ASP.NET Core runtime starts up.

Run the command shown in Listing 6-24 in the ExampleApp folder to confirm the state of the application.

Listing 6-24. Inspecting the Application

```
docker-compose ps
```

The docker-compose ps command shows the running containers that have been created from the compose file and will produce output like this:

```
Name                         Command                      State      Ports
--------------------------------------------------------------------------------------
exampleapp_dbinit_1          /bin/sh -c ./wait-for-it.s ...  Exit 0
exampleapp_loadbalancer_1    dockercloud-haproxy             Up         1936/tcp,
                                                                        443/tcp,
                                                        0.0.0.0:3000->80/tcp
exampleapp_mvc_1             /bin/sh -c ./wait-for-it.s ...  Up         80/tcp
exampleapp_mvc_2             /bin/sh -c ./wait-for-it.s ...  Up         80/tcp
exampleapp_mvc_3             /bin/sh -c ./wait-for-it.s ...  Up         80/tcp
exampleapp_mvc_4             /bin/sh -c ./wait-for-it.s ...  Up         80/tcp
exampleapp_mysql_1           docker-entrypoint.sh mysqld     Up         3306/tcp
```

You can see that the dbinit container has exited, which was intentional after checking and preparing the database. There are six running containers: the database, four MVC containers, and the load balancer.

The image used for the load balancer service configures HAProxy to respond to changes in the number of containers in the service specified by the link configuration property in the compose file. This property was set to mvc in Listing 6-18, which means the load balancer automatically starts directing HTTP requests to mvc containers when they are created, without the need for any configuration changes.

Open a new browser tab and request http://localhost:3000. Reload the browser to send additional HTTP requests to the load balancer, which will be distributed between the MVC containers. The output in the command prompt used to start the mvc service will indicate which container has handled the request, and you will see different host names displayed in the responses, as shown in Figure 6-2.

Figure 6-2. *Dynamically configuring the load balancer*

■ **Tip**   Not all containers are suitable for scaling up. The MySQL container cannot be scaled up, for example, because the mysql service specifies a Docker volume for the data files and MySQL doesn't support two database processes sharing the same files. Containers that rely on port mappings to the host operating system, like the load balancer, can't be scaled up either because only the first container will be able to use the port.

Run the command shown in Listing 6-25 in the ExampleApp folder to scale down the number of MVC application containers to one.

Listing 6-25. Scaling Down the MVC Containers

```
docker-compose scale mvc=1
```

All the HTTP requests received by the load balancer will be directed to the remaining MVC container.

Stopping the Application

Run the command shown in Listing 6-26 in the ExampleApp folder to stop all the containers.

Listing 6-26. Stopping the Application Containers

```
docker-compose stop
```

Finally, run the command shown in Listing 6-27 in the ExampleApp folder to remove the containers, networks, and volumes. (Be careful when using the -v flag in production systems.)

Listing 6-27. Removing the Application Components

```
docker-compose down -v
```

Summary

In this chapter, I explained how a compose file can be used to describe a complex application, including the containers it requires, the volumes they depend on, and the software-defined networks that connect them. I demonstrated how a complex application can be brought to life using the docker-compose command and how the number of containers in an application can be scaled up and down as needed. In the next chapter, I explain how to use a Docker swarm, which allows a containerized application to be deployed across multiple servers that have been clustered together.

CHAPTER 7

■ ■ ■

Docker Swarms

In the previous chapter, I demonstrated how to manage a complex application on a single server using Docker Compose. In this chapter, I explain how to scale up applications so they run on multiple servers, using a *Docker swarm*.

A Docker swarm is a cluster of servers that run the Docker engine. Each server in a swarm is known as a node, of which there are two types. Manager nodes are used to orchestrate *services*, which are the desired state for containerized applications, such as the example ASP.NET Core MVC application or MySQL. A service describes how many containers should be created and which nodes in the cluster should run them. This is known as the service's desired state.

Manager nodes perform their orchestration by managing the other type of node: worker nodes. A worker is responsible for running the containers delivering the functionality specified by the service. When a container or a worker node fails, the manager node will automatically detect the change and try to return to the desired state by starting additional containers on other nodes. To make this process simpler, a Docker swarm supports software-defined networks that can span the nodes in a cluster and routes requests between the containers connected to the network. Table 7-1 puts Docker swarms in context.

SWARMS REQUIRE LINUX

The clustering of nodes in a swarm is achieved using features that are specific to Linux. At the time of writing, only Linux servers can be clustered together to create a swarm. Neither Windows nor macOS supports the cluster features and cannot be used for the examples in this chapter, although Microsoft has plans to introduce the required features for Windows.

If you don't have your own Linux servers, you can create Linux virtual machines to see how swarms work, either locally or on public clouds such as Microsoft Azure or Amazon Web Services. Many public cloud services also have direct support for swarms, such as the Azure Container Service.

Alternatively, you can use Docker Cloud, which is a service provided by Docker that orchestrates the deployment and management of Docker services on public cloud services, including Azure and AWS. The Docker Cloud service is a paid-for service and requires an account on at least one of the cloud providers. There are free tiers available, but they place limits on the number of nodes you can include in your swarm.

© Adam Freeman 2017
A. Freeman, *Essential Docker for ASP.NET Core MVC*, DOI 10.1007/978-1-4842-2778-7_7

Table 7-1. *Putting Swarms in Context*

Question	Answer
What is it?	A Docker swarm is a cluster of servers that run the containers in an application in a coordinated manner.
Why is it useful?	A swarm allows an application to scale beyond a single server, making an application more tolerant to the failure of individual containers.
How is it used?	A swarm consists of manager and worker nodes. The manager nodes are responsible for managing the containers in the application, deciding which workers will run them, and ensuring that they are running.
Are there any pitfalls or limitations?	It is important to exclude components that receive external network connections (such as load balancers) from the swarm; otherwise, they will be subject to the ingress load balancing feature, which is described in this chapter.
Are there any alternatives?	There are several alternatives to Docker swarms. The most successful are Kubernetes (`https://kubernetes.io`), which was originally developed by Google, and Mesos (`http://mesos.apache.org`), which is an Apache Software Foundation Project. Both Kubernetes and Mesos provide support for working with Docker containers. Kubernetes, in particular, is well-established and well-supported. Docker swarms are relatively new but have the advantage of being integrated into the Docker runtime and have the backing of Microsoft, which is important for ASP. NET Core MVC projects.

Table 7-2 summarizes this chapter.

Table 7-2. *Chapter Summary*

Problem	Solution	Listing
Create a swarm	Run `docker swarm init` on the manager node and then run the command shown in the output on each of the workers	1–3
Differentiate worker nodes	Assign the node a label	4
Create a network in the swarm	Use the `docker network create` command with the `-d` argument set to `overlay`	5
Deploy a service to a swarm	Use the `docker service create` command	6, 11–14
Examine a service	Use the `docker service ps` or `docker service ls` command	7, 15, 16, 22, 38
Modify a service	Use the `docker service update` command	8–10, 23, 30, 33
Remove a service	Use the `docker service rm` command	19
Deploy services using a compose file	Use the `deploy` keyword to describe the service in the compose file and then use the `docker stack deploy` command	20, 21, 37

(continued)

Table 7-2. (*continued*)

Problem	Solution	Listing
Change the number of containers in a service	Use the docker `service scale` command	26, 27, 34
Change the status of a node in the cluster	Use the docker `node update` command	28, 29
Remove the services described in a compose file	Use the docker `stack rm` command	35
Deploy one container in a service on each node in a swarm	Set mode to global in the compose file	36

Preparing for This Chapter

This chapter depends on the ExampleApp MVC project created in Chapter 3 and modified in the chapters since. If you don't want to work through the process of creating the example, you can get the project as part of the free source code download that accompanies this book. See the apress.com page for this book.

To ensure that there is no conflict with examples from previous chapters, run the commands shown in Listing 7-1 to remove the Docker containers, networks, and volumes. Ignore any errors or warnings these commands produce.

Listing 7-1. Removing the Containers, Networks, and Volumes

```
docker rm -f $(docker ps -aq)
docker network rm $(docker network ls -q)
docker volume rm $(docker volume ls -q)
```

Preparing the Swarm

In this chapter, I create a swarm that contains five nodes or servers. Working with a swarm means referring to the servers in the cluster by name, and to make the examples easier to follow, the servers are described in Table 7-3. The configuration that I have chosen for my swarm is typical for a small cluster. As the number of worker nodes increases, a swarm should include additional manager nodes.

■ **Note**   The manager node in my swarm runs Ubuntu. The worker nodes all run CoreOS Container Linux, which is a lightweight Linux distribution specifically intended for running application containers and that includes Docker as part of its standard build. CoreOS is supported by the main cloud platforms, including Microsoft Azure, Amazon Web Services, and Google Cloud, and it makes a good target operating system for working with Docker swarms. See http://coreos.com for details.

Table 7-3. *The Hosts in the Example Swarm*

Name	Description
manager	This is the manager node, which will be responsible for orchestrating the services in the swarm. It is also where I copied the ExampleApp folder that contains the example application and the configuration files and is where almost all the commands in this chapter are run. This server will also run the load balancer that will receive HTTP requests and distribute them to the containers running the MVC application.
dbhost	This is a worker node that will be dedicated to running the MySQL container.
worker1	This is a worker node that will run MVC application containers.
worker2	This is a worker node that will run MVC application containers.
worker3	This is a worker node that will run MVC application containers.

Creating the Swarm

A swarm is created on the manager node, which generates a key that can then be used by the workers to join the swarm. Run the command shown in Listing 7-2 on the manager node to create a swarm.

Listing 7-2. Creating a Swarm

```
docker swarm init
```

The output gives you the instructions for associating the other nodes with the swarm, with the command you must run on each node in the swarm marked in bold.

```
Swarm initialized: current node (u9np4ffl3aqao9c3c2bnuzgqm) is now a manager.

To add a worker to this swarm, run the following command:
```

**docker swarm join **
    --token SWMTKN-1-61tskndg374fkvoa7fl0c8d57w2zvku9hzvqpfmojqhw51dlj9-
**c1cwiu06s4bfjcj0ekf9lh8uv **
        172.16.0.5:2377

```
To add a manager to this swarm, run 'docker swarm join-token manager' and follow the
instructions.
```

You will see a different token and a different network value or format of network address based on the configuration of your manager node. Run the command indicated in the output on each worker in your swarm. As the command runs successfully, you will see the following message displayed on each worker:

```
...
This node joined a swarm as a worker
...
```

This is the only command that is run on the worker nodes. Once a node is part of a swarm, it is controlled using the manager node. All the remaining examples in this chapter are carried out on the manager node.

When you have added all the nodes to the swarm, run the command in Listing 7-3 on the manager to examine the swarm.

Listing 7-3. Examining the Nodes in the Swarm

```
docker node ls
```

The output from this command will show all the nodes in the swarm (the asterisk indicates the node you are working on).

```
ID                                  HOSTNAME  STATUS  AVAILABILITY  MANAGER STATUS
136uyxxgnldhurrgtj2o9cr0h *         manager   Ready   Active        Leader
e7wwq0oghzx16g9jkz9642nws           dbhost    Ready   Active
gmpyip1ms88kiu5inlwytz2qd           worker2   Ready   Active
o479m45qwi6vlq8pmgas21e96           worker3   Ready   Active
yl9ajlaku5du3hpmsbaf33dyh           worker1   Ready   Active
```

■ **Tip**   If you want to leave a swarm, then run the `docker swarm leave` command on the node. For manager nodes, use the `docker swarm leave --force` command.

Labeling Swarm Nodes

Nodes in a swarm can be assigned labels that can be used to control the types of container they run. For this example, I am going to use labels to differentiate between the node that will be responsible for running the database and the nodes that will be responsible for the MVC application. Run the commands shown in Listing 7-4 on the manager node to assign labels to the worker nodes in the swarm, assigning them the type label and setting its value to mvc. Labels are arbitrary and can be assigned in any way that helps make sense of your swarm and the application running on it: the type label I have used here and the value mvc have no special meaning to Docker.

Listing 7-4. Assigning Labels to the Nodes in the Swarm

```
docker node update --label-add type=mvc worker1
docker node update --label-add type=mvc worker2
docker node update --label-add type=mvc worker3
```

Manually Deploying Services on a Swarm

The simplest way to use a swarm is to describe the application in a compose file, as demonstrated in the *"Deploying to a Swarm Using a Compose File"* section. But to understand what happens behind the scenes, it helps to go through the process of deploying an application manually, even though this is a process that requires careful attention to detail to type complex commands correctly. (For this reason, it is something that you should do only to understand how swarms work and not in production.)

Creating the Software-Defined Networks

Docker supports software-defined networks that connect the nodes in a swarm, allowing containers to seamlessly communicate across the swarm. To create the network for the example application, run the command shown in Listing 7-5 on the manager node.

Listing 7-5. Creating the Software-Defined Networks

```
docker network create -d overlay swarm_backend
```

The -d argument specifies the type of software-defined network, which is set to overlay when creating a network that will span the servers in the swarm. I have prefixed the network name with swarm_ to differentiate it from earlier examples; this is a not a requirement for real projects.

■ **Tip**　There is only one network in this example because the communication between the load balancer and the MVC application will occur outside the swarm, as explained in the "*Creating the Load Balancer*" section.

The effect of the command in Listing 7-5 is to create a software-defined network that connects together all the nodes in the swarm, as illustrated by Figure 7-1.

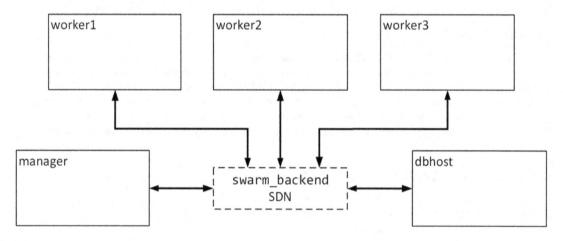

Figure 7-1.　*Creating a swarm network*

Creating the Database Service

Deploying and configuring a database in a swarm can be awkward because the nature of databases is somewhat opposed to the nature of swarms. The services that can take most advantage of the swarm features are the ones that can easily be replicated by starting new containers and that can be easily moved between nodes in the cluster.

Databases don't fit well into this model: there tends to be a small number of database services in an application (often just one instance), they rely on data files that cannot be easily transported to other nodes in the cluster, and there can be substantial initialization and shutdown processes that preserve data integrity.

For these reasons, you may prefer to set up your database server outside of the swarm and configure your MVC application containers to make queries over the physical network that connects your servers. Since this is a book about Docker, I am going to demonstrate how to deploy the database within the swarm cluster, even though there will be only one container in the service and it will be deployed to a specific node. This will let me demonstrate some useful Docker features, even though it is not a suitable approach for all projects.

Run the command shown in Listing 7-6 on the manager node to create the MySQL service. (Enter the command on a single line.)

Listing 7-6. Creating the Database Service

```
docker service create --name mysql
    --mount type=volume,source=productdata,destination=/var/lib/mysql
    --constraint "node.hostname == dbhost" --replicas 1 --network swarm_backend
    -e MYSQL_ROOT_PASSWORD=mysecret -e bind-address=0.0.0.0 mysql:8.0.0
```

Services are created using the `docker service create` command, with the arguments telling Docker how the service should be deployed. For MySQL, I want to create a single container with a persistent data volume on the dbhost swarm node, using the arguments described in Table 7-4.

Table 7-4. *The Arguments Used to Create the MySQL Service*

Name	Description
`--name`	This argument sets the name for the service, which is `mysql` in this example.
`--mount`	This argument is used to specify the volumes that will be used by the containers created by the service. In this example, a volume called `productdata` will be used to provide content for the `/var/lib/sql` directory.
`--constraint`	This argument is used to restrict the nodes in the swarm where containers for the services can run, as described in the "Using Swarm Constraints" sidebar. In this example, containers for this service can run only on the node whose host name is dbhost.
`--replicas`	This argument is used to specify the desired number of containers that should be run for this service. In this example, one container is specified, which is typical for databases.
`--network`	This argument is used to specify the software-defined networks to which containers created for this service will be attached. In this example, the containers will be connected to the `swarm_backend` network.
`-e`	This argument is used to specify environment variables that will be used to configure containers created for this service. The example uses the same MySQL variables introduced in Chapter 5.

Volumes are handled differently in swarms, and care must be taken. The `--mount` argument used in Listing 7-6 will create a new volume called `productdata` and use it for the container specified in the service. But the volume is specific to the swarm node where the service starts the container and will not migrate if the container is stopped and moved to another node in the swarm.

The constraint in the command in Listing 7-6 means that the manager can achieve the desired state for the `mysql` service only by creating a container on the dbhost node. Only one replica has been specified, which means that a single database container is started on dbhost, connected to the `swarm_backend` network, as shown in Figure 7-2.

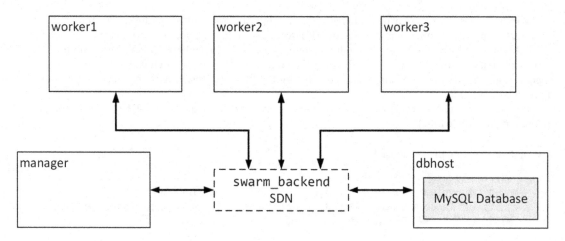

Figure 7-2. *Starting the database service*

It can take a while for the database service to start, as the image is downloaded from the Docker Hub to the worker node. Keep track of the progress of the service by running the command shown in Listing 7-7 on the manager node.

Listing 7-7. Monitoring a Docker Service

```
docker service ps mysql
```

The docker service ps command lists the containers that are running in the swarm for a service. As the service is being prepared, you will see output like this:

```
...
ID              NAME        IMAGE        NODE     DESIRED STATE  CURRENT STATE
wzly7bxjxaqg  mysql.1  mysql:8.0.0  dbhost   Running        Preparing
...
```

The DESIRED STATE column shows the state that Docker is working toward for the container, while the CURRENT STATE column shows how it is progressing. Once the container has started, the output of the docker service ps command will show that the container is in the target state, like this:

```
...
ID              NAME        IMAGE        NODE     DESIRED STATE  CURRENT STATE
wzly7bxjxaqg  mysql.1  mysql:8.0.0  dbhost   Running        Running
...
```

USING SWARM CONSTRAINTS

Most real projects will be deployed into clusters where some nodes have a specific role, such as running the database, typically because they have more capable or specialized hardware.

When you deploy a service into a swarm, you can control which nodes will be assigned containers by specifying constraints. The manager will only assign containers to nodes that meet the constraints specified for the service.

There are several different ways that a service can be constrained. The first is they can be deployed to a specific node, identified using its host name. This is the approach I took with the database in Listing 7-6:

```
...
--constraint "node.hostname == dbhost"
...
```

If you want to deploy a service so that it runs only on nodes of a specific type, then you can use a constraint like this:

```
...
--constraint "node.role == manager"
...
```

You can also restrict deployment to nodes that have been assigned a specific label. I assigned labels to three of the worker nodes in Listing 7-4, and I use this label when deploying the service for the MVC application in Listing 7-14, using a constraint like this:

```
...
--constraint "node.labels.type==mvc"
...
```

Labels are the most flexible way to constrain a service because you can assign any label you need to any label in the swarm.

Preparing the Database

When I described the application using a Docker Compose file in Chapter 6, I was able to include a container that was dedicated to initializing the database, after which it would exit. It is possible to arrange this kind of setup in a swarm, but there is a more interesting feature available that provides useful insight into how swarms function. To prepare the database, I am going to temporarily map the database's port 3306 so that it can be accessed through the host operating system and use this to perform the initialization. Bear with me; this is more interesting than it may sound.

Run the command shown in Listing 7-8 on the manager node to update the database service. (The command is run on the manager node, even though the container is running on a worker. Remember that the manager node is always used to configure the services running on a cluster.)

Listing 7-8. Updating the Database Service

```
docker service update --publish-add 3306:3306 mysql
```

The docker service update command is used to change the configuration of services after they have been created. You can change almost any aspect of the service including defining new mapped ports with the --publish-add argument. This command makes port 3306 available outside of the swarm for the mysql service. Docker applies the change across the swarm, ensuring consistency across all the containers that are part of the service.

When you expose a port from a service, Docker maps it to the host operating systems on all the nodes in the swarm, using a feature called *ingress load balancing*. This means that *any* request to port 3306 received on *any* node in the swarm will be received by Docker and sent to one of the containers in the service whose port was mapped.

For the mysql service, there is only a single container, which is running on the dbhost node, and so any request sent to port 3306 on the manager, worker1, worker2, worker3, and dbhost nodes will be received by MySQL on port 3306 inside the container running on the dbhost node. When there are multiple containers in a service, Docker will load balance the requests so that they are distributed between the containers.

The ingress load balancing feature simplifies the process of preparing the database. Run the commands shown in Listing 7-9 in the ExampleApp folder on the manager node.

Listing 7-9. Preparing the Database in the Swarm

```
dotnet restore
dotnet run --INITDB=true
```

When the .NET application runs, the INITDB argument selects the database initialization mode, rather than starting ASP.NET Core. Since all the nodes in the swarm map port 3306 to the database service, it doesn't matter which host name is used to configure the database. The application defaults to localhost when no other host name is supplied, which means that the connection from Entity Framework Core is made to port 3306 on the manager node, and the swarm ensures that it is channeled to port 3306 on the dbhost node so that it can be received by MySQL, as illustrated by Figure 7-3.

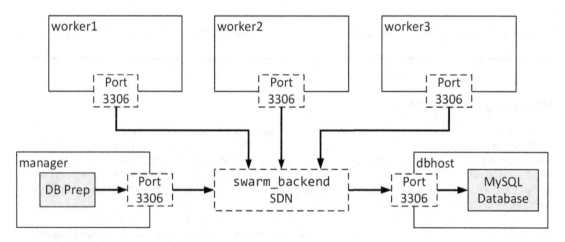

Figure 7-3. *Using ingress load balancing to prepare the database*

It doesn't matter which host in the cluster the database preparation application connects to because any request to port 3306 on any node will be channeled to the container running on dbhost, ensuring that the database is correctly prepared for the application. Put another way, a connection sent to port 3306 on the manager node is effectively the same as a connection to port 3306 on the dbhost node.

The application will produce the following results, showing that the database migrations have been applied to create the schema and that the seed data has been added:

```
...
Preparing Database...
Applying Migrations...
Creating Seed Data...
Database Preparation Complete
...
```

■ **Tip** If you see an error when you use the dotnet run command, then wait a couple of minutes to give Docker time to update the service so that port 3306 is available and try again. If you see an error telling you that the Products table already exists, then you may have already initialized the database: Entity Framework Core migrations have to be applied only once. If you want to repeat the initialization, delete the productdata volume on the dbhost worker node, restart the mysql service, expose port 3306, and run the commands in Listing 7-9 again.

Once you have prepared the database, run the command shown in Listing 7-10 on the manager node to disable ingress load balancing for port 3306 so that the database returns to being accessible only through the swarm_backend software-defined network.

Listing 7-10. Disabling the Port Mapping

```
docker service update --publish-rm 3306:3306 mysql
```

Creating the MVC Application Service

The MVC application is better suited to deployment in a swarm than the database: the application is self-contained, it doesn't matter which nodes run the application, and multiple instances of the MVC application can be created without conflicting with one another.

The manager node in a swarm doesn't distribute the images required for a service to the worker nodes, which means that the image used to create a service must be published to a repository, such as the Docker Hub, so that the nodes in the swarm can get the data they require to create containers.

Run the commands shown in Listing 7-11 in the manager node's ExampleApp folder to prepare the application for deployment.

Listing 7-11. Preparing the MVC Application for Deployment as a Service

```
dotnet publish --framework netcoreapp1.1 --configuration Release --output dist
docker build . -t apress/exampleapp:swarm-1.0 -f Dockerfile
```

You will need to change the name of the image created by the docker build command to replace apress with your Docker Hub account. So, if your account name is bobsmith, then your image tag should be bobsmith/exampleapp:swarm-1.0.

The dotnet publish command ensures that recent changes made to the MVC application will be included in the Docker image that is created by the docker build command.

The tag for the MVC application image includes a variation, which is swarm-1.0. (You don't have to include swarm in the tags for your images. I have done this so that the image for this example can coexist with those from earlier chapters.)

■ **Tip**　It is always a good idea to use specific versions of images when creating services rather than relying on the :latest version, which may change unexpectedly during the life of the application. Later in the chapter, I explain how to upgrade an application that is used in a service, which also requires an image tag with a version.

Run the commands shown in Listing 7-12 in the ExampleApp folder of the manager node to authenticate with the Docker Hub using the credentials you created in Chapter 4.

Listing 7-12. Authenticating with Docker Hub

```
docker login -u <yourUsername> -p <yourPassword>
```

Run the command shown in Listing 7-13 on the manager node to push the image to the repository. Don't forget to change the name of the image for the docker push command to replace apress with your Docker Hub account.

Listing 7-13. Pushing the MVC Image to the Repository

```
docker push apress/exampleapp:swarm-1.0
```

Once the image has been pushed to the repository, run the command shown in Listing 7-14 on the manager node to create the service for the MVC application. Enter the command on a single line.

Listing 7-14. Creating the MVC Application Service

```
docker service create --name mvcapp --constraint "node.labels.type==mvc"
    --replicas 5 --network swarm_backend -p 3000:80
    -e DBHOST=mysql apress/exampleapp:swarm-1.0
```

This command tells Docker to create a service for the MVC application that consists of five containers, which can be run only on nodes that have been assigned the type label with a value of mvc. Access to the containers in the service will be through the port published using the -p argument, which configures the ingress load balancing feature described in the previous section.

Notice that the DBHOST environment variable, which specifies the name of the database server for the Entity Framework Core connection string, is set to mysql. Within a swarm, Docker creates host names that provide access to the ingress load balancing feature for each service that is created. This means Entity Framework Core can open a connection to mysql and rely on Docker to channel that connection to one of the containers that provides the mysql service. There is only one container in the mysql service, but Docker will load balance between containers if there is more than one available.

The complete set of arguments used to create the MVC application service is described in Table 7-5.

Table 7-5. *The Arguments Used to Create the MVC Service*

Name	Description
--name	This argument is used to set the name for the service, which is mvcapp in this example.
--constraint	This argument is used to restrict the nodes where containers for this service will run, as described in the *"Using Swarm Constraints"* sidebar. For this example, the containers will run only on the nodes assigned the mvc label in Listing 7-4.
--replicas	This argument specifies the desired number of containers that will run for this service. For this example, five containers are specified.
--network	This argument specifies the software-defined networks that the containers for this service will be connected to. For this example, the containers will be connected to the swarm_backend service.
-p	This argument exposes a port inside the containers created for this service to ingress load balancing features. Requests sent to the specified port will be directed to one of the service containers. In this example, requests sent to port 3000 on any node in the cluster will be directed to port 80 inside one of the mvc containers.
-e	This argument sets an environment variable when containers are created for the service. In this example, the DBHOST variable is set in order to provide the host name that Entity Framework Core needs to connect to the database. The host name is set to the name of the database service, which takes advantage of the ingress load balancing feature.

It will take Docker a moment to set up the containers. You can check the progress by running the command shown in Listing 7-15 on the manager node.

Listing 7-15. Checking Service Status

```
docker service ls
```

The results from the docker service ls command show a summary of the services that have been created on the swarm and the status of each of them. When Docker has created all the containers required for the MVC application service, the REPLICAS column in the docker service ls output will show 5/5, indicating that Docker has created all five containers and has reached the desired state for the service, as follows:

```
ID              NAME      MODE        REPLICAS  IMAGE
4kf7xsym2vc5    mvcapp    replicated  5/5       apress/exampleapp:swarm-1.0
j2v5gdqzu1di    mysql     replicated  1/1       mysql:8.0.0
```

Docker is responsible for allocating the containers required for the service to worker nodes. Run the command shown in Listing 7-16 on the manager to see which nodes in the containers within the service have been deployed to.

Listing 7-16. Examining the Containers in a Service

```
docker service ps mvcapp
```

131

The docker service ps command produces a list of all the containers running in a service. Here is the output from my setup, formatted to fit on the page and with only the most useful columns shown:

```
ID              NAME        NODE      DESIRED STATE    CURRENT STATE
7jd1yop74mxfy   mvcapp.1    worker1   Running          Running
cse2cyutpvxh9   mvcapp.2    worker2   Running          Running
5r9y800jugey8   mvcapp.3    worker1   Running          Running
cktdzf0ypzcpt   mvcapp.4    worker3   Running          Running
5esdl2d3jd1ee   mvcapp.5    worker2   Running          Running
```

In this example, there are five containers running on three workers, which means that some worker nodes are running multiple containers, as illustrated in Figure 7-4.

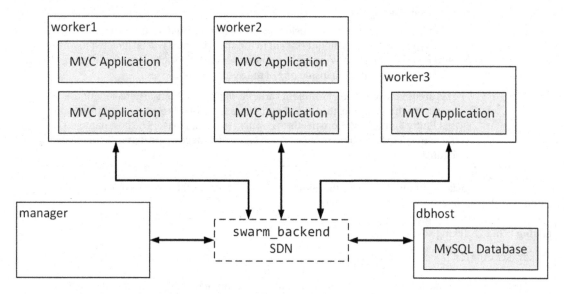

Figure 7-4. *Deploying the ASP.NET Core MVC application service*

If you reboot a worker node, disconnect it from the network, or just stop a container on a worker, the swarm manager will return the service to its desired state by creating additional containers on the other nodes.

Testing the MVC Application Service

The configuration of the MVC application service included a port mapping so that HTTP requests received on port 3000 of any node in the swarm will be sent to port 80 inside one of the MVC containers. Since there are multiple MVC containers, the ingress load balancing feature will distribute the requests between them.

You can see how the requests are distributed by opening a new browser window and requesting the URL for port 3000 on any of the swarm nodes, including the manager node. The URL in my setup is http://manager:3000. Keep reloading the page and you will see that the container name included in the response will change, as shown in Figure 7-5. Docker doesn't make any promises about how requests are distributed, and you may have to reload the page a few times before you see a different container name. If you don't see any change in the name, then wait a few minutes and reload the page, try starting a second browser, or make a request from a different IP address.

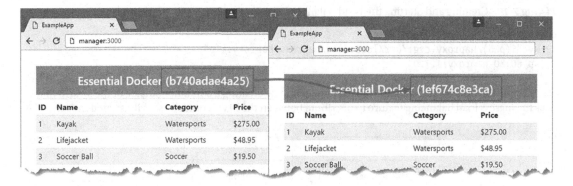

Figure 7-5. *Testing the MVC service through the mesh routing feature*

Creating the Load Balancer

Although you could rely on the ingress load balancing feature to handle HTTP requests from users, the convention is to deploy a load balancer so that there is a single point of entry to the application from the outside world.

It is important not to deploy the load balancer as a service in the swarm since that would mean the Docker ingress load balancing system would receive the HTTP requests from the outside world and then distribute them over the software-defined network to one or more containers, which would use ingress load balancing to target one of the MVC containers.

Instead, I am going to run the HAProxy application I used in earlier examples in a separate container on the manager node. This container will use a regular port mapping to the host operating system to receive HTTP requests and forward them to the MVC application containers through the swarm mesh network. Listing 7-17 shows the change required to the haproxy.cfg file to configure the load balancer.

Listing 7-17. Configuring the Load Balancer in the haproxy.cfg File

```
defaults
    timeout connect 5000
    timeout client  50000
    timeout server  50000

frontend localnodes
    bind *:80
    mode http
    default_backend mvc

backend mvc
    mode http
    balance roundrobin
    server mvc1 manager:3000
```

There are lots of ways to configure the load balancer, but the approach I use is to forward requests to the ingress load-balanced port on the local machine so that HAProxy doesn't have to be configured with the details of the worker nodes. Run the command shown in Listing 7-18 on the manager node to create a new load balancer container that uses the configuration file from Listing 7-17. (Enter the command on a single line.)

Listing 7-18. Creating and Starting the Load Balancer Container

```
docker run -d --name loadbalancer
  -v "$(pwd)/haproxy.cfg:/usr/local/etc/haproxy/haproxy.cfg"
  -p 80:80 haproxy:1.7.0
```

Adding the load balancer completes the application by creating a container outside of the swarm that uses the ingress load balancing feature to distribute between the MVC containers, as illustrated in Figure 7-6.

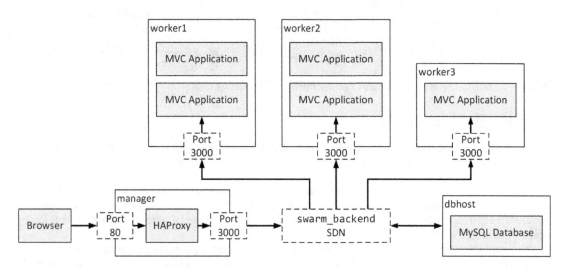

Figure 7-6. *Completing the application*

You can test the application by using the browser to request port 80 on the manager node, which means using the URL http://manager in my setup. The HTTP request is fed to the HAProxy load balancer through the port 80 mapping on the manager node, which then directs the request to port 3000, relying on the ingress load balancing feature to distribute the request to the MVC application containers.

Reloading the web page will show that different MVC application containers are being used to handle the requests, although you may have to wait for a moment before reloading (or use a different browser) to see the change illustrated in Figure 7-7.

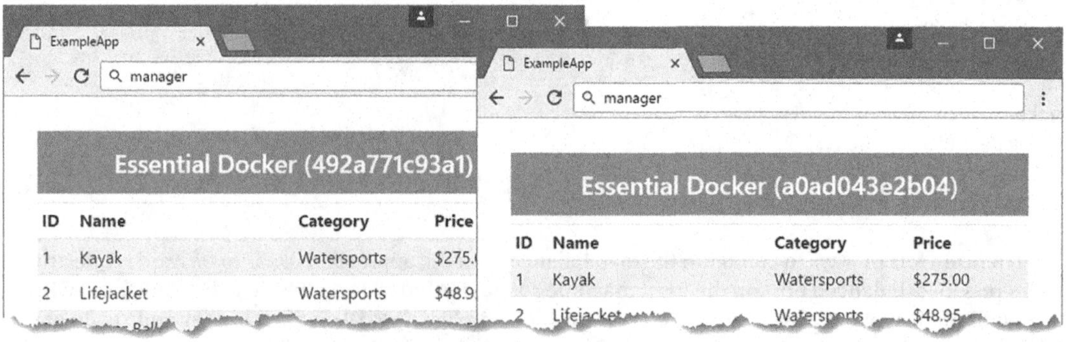

Figure 7-7. *Making requests through a load balancer*

■ **Tip** If you don't get the expected results, use the `docker logs loadbalancer` command to inspect the output from the load balancer container for errors. Resolve the problem, use `docker rm -f loadbalancer` to remove the container, and run the command in Listing 7-18 again.

Removing the Service from the Swarm

To remove the service from the cluster, run the commands shown in Listing 7-19 on the manager node.

Listing 7-19. Removing Docker Services

```
docker service rm mvcapp
docker service rm mysql
docker rm -f loadbalancer
docker network rm swarm_backend
```

Deploying to a Swarm Using a Compose File

Although you can deploy an application to a swarm using the commands described in the previous section, it is easier to include the information in a compose file and let Docker take care of the deployment. Add a file called `docker-compose-swarm.yml` in the ExampleApp folder of the manager node and add the configuration shown in Listing 7-20.

Listing 7-20. The Contents of docker-compose-swarm.yml in the ExampleApp Folder

```
version: "3"

volumes:
  productdata_swarm:

networks:
  backend:

services:

  mysql:
    image: "mysql:8.0.0"
    volumes:
      - productdata_swarm:/var/lib/mysql
    networks:
      - backend
    environment:
      - MYSQL_ROOT_PASSWORD=mysecret
      - bind-address=0.0.0.0
    deploy:
      replicas: 1
      placement:
        constraints:
          - node.hostname == dbhost
```

135

```
mvc:
  image: "apress/exampleapp:swarm-1.0"
  networks:
    - backend
  environment:
    - DBHOST=mysql
  ports:
    - 3000:80
  deploy:
    replicas: 5
    placement:
      constraints:
      - node.labels.type == mvc
```

A compose file that targets a swarm describes the desired state for a service using the deploy configuration section, which is described in Table 7-6.

Table 7-6. *The Deployment Configuration Options in the Compose File*

Name	Description
deploy	This configuration section is used to configure the desired state for the service when it is deployed on the cluster.
replicas	This setting is used to specify how many instances of a container are required for a service. In this example, there will be one container for the database and five containers for the ASP.NET Core MVC application.
placement	This configuration section is used to configure the placement of the containers for the service.
constraints	This setting specifies constrains for locating the containers in the swarm. In this example, the database container will run only on the dbhost node, and the MVC application containers will run on the nodes that were labeled in Listing 7-4.

Some Docker Compose features are not supported when deploying services to a swarm, such as the build configuration section (services must use images) and the depend_on setting. The compose file should contain only those services that you want to deploy to the cluster. The file in Listing 7-20, for example, omits details of the database initialization and load balancer containers, which will be created on the manager node, outside of the swarm.

Performing the Deployment

Run the command shown in Listing 7-21 in the ExampleApp folder on the manager node to deploy the services described in the new compose file.

Listing 7-21. Deploying Services from a Compose File

```
docker stack deploy --compose-file docker-compose-swarm.yml exampleapp
```

A stack is the term that Docker uses to describe a collection of services that make up an application. The docker stack deploy command creates a stack using the information in the compose file, using the arguments described in Table 7-7.

Table 7-7. *The Arguments Used for the Docker Stack Deploy Command*

Name	Description
--compose-file	The --compose-file argument specifies the compose file that contains the details of the services in the stack. An alternative description file, called a bundle, can also be used.
exampleapp	The final argument to the docker stack deploy command is the name that will be assigned to the stack and that is used to prefix the names of the containers, volumes, and software-defined networks that are created for the stack.

As Docker processes the compose file, it will create the components that application requires, producing output like this:

```
...
Creating network exampleapp_backend
Creating service exampleapp_mvc
Creating service exampleapp_mysql
...
```

The software-defined network and the containers for the database and the MVC application will be started. The docker service commands described earlier in the chapter can be used to inspect the services that have been created. Run the commands shown in Listing 7-22 on the manager node.

Listing 7-22. Inspecting the Services

```
docker service ls
docker service ps exampleapp_mvc
```

The docker service ls command lists the services that have been deployed to the swarm. The second command details the containers that have been created for the exampleapp_mvc service. The name of the service combines the final argument given to the docker stack deploy command in Listing 7-21 and the name of the service defined in the compose file in Listing 7-20.

Preparing the Database

The process for preparing the database hasn't changed. Run the command in Listing 7-23 to expose port 3306 via the ingress load balancer so that the database can be reached outside of the software-defined network defined in the compose file.

Listing 7-23. Exposing the Database Port

```
docker service update --publish-add 3306:3306 exampleapp_mysql
```

Give Docker a minute to perform the update and then run the command shown in Listing 7-24 in the ExampleApp folder of the manager node to apply the Entity Framework Core migration and create the seed data. (If you get a database connection error, then wait a little longer and try again.)

Listing 7-24. Initializing the Database

```
dotnet run --INITDB=true
```

Creating the Deployment Load Balancer

The final step is to create the load balancer, which is outside of the swarm for the reasons described earlier in the chapter. Run the command shown in Listing 7-25 in the ExampleApp folder of the manager node to create the load balancer container. This container isn't part of the cluster but relies on the ingress load balancing feature to distribute HTTP requests to the MVC application containers. (Enter the command on a single line.)

Listing 7-25. Creating the Load Balancer

```
docker run -d --name stack_loadbalancer
  -v "$(pwd)/haproxy.cfg:/usr/local/etc/haproxy/haproxy.cfg" -p 80:80 haproxy:1.7.0
```

Once the load balancer has started, you can test the application by opening a new browser window and requesting port 80 on the manager node. For me, this means the URL is http://manager. The configuration of the application is just the same as when each component was created manually, but using the compose file simplifies the commands used for deployment.

Managing the Swarm

To a certain extent, a swarm is self-managing because when a container or a node crashes, the manager will try to create additional containers to return to the desired state of the services. Even so, there are times when you will want to change the way that a swarm behaves, which you can do using the features described in the sections that follow.

Scaling Services

One of the most common changes to a service is to alter the number of containers to better suit the application's workload. Run the command shown in Listing 7-26 on the manager node to alter the number of containers in the MVC application service.

Listing 7-26. Changing the Number of Containers

```
docker service scale exampleapp_mvc=3
```

The docker service scale command is used to change the desired state of the service. This command tells Docker to reduce the number of containers in the mvc service to 3. It will take a moment for the change to take effect, but once Docker has adjusted the service, the new configuration can be seen by running the docker service ls command, which will produce a response like this:

```
ID              NAME              MODE         REPLICAS  IMAGE
41sdv2rpppyr    exampleapp_mysql  replicated   1/1       mysql:8.0.0
mchxy13rn37z    exampleapp_mvc    replicated   3/3       apress/exampleapp:swarm-1.0
```

Run the command shown in Listing 7-27 on the manager node to return the service to its original number of containers.

Listing 7-27. Returning to the Original Scale

```
docker service scale exampleapp_mvc=5
```

Taking Nodes Out of Service

There will be times when you need to take a node out of the swarm, perhaps to perform an upgrade or some other kind of maintenance. You could just disconnect the node and let the manager detect the change and rebalance the service, but a more orderly approach is to drain a node in the swarm. Draining a node takes it out of service and causes the manager to redistribute its containers to other nodes, at which point it can be shut down without interrupting service delivery. Run the command shown in Listing 7-28 on the manager node to drain the worker2 node.

Listing 7-28. Draining a Node

```
docker node update --availability drain worker2
```

In addition to labeling nodes, as shown in Listing 7-4, the docker node update command can be used with the --availability argument to change the status of nodes in a swarm. There are three types of availability, as described in Table 7-8.

Table 7-8. *The Swarm Node Availability Types*

Name	Description
active	This is the default availability. The manager is free to assign new containers to the node, and any existing containers continue running indefinitely.
pause	In this mode, the existing containers on the node will continue to run, but the manager won't assign any new containers.
drain	In this mode, existing containers will be stopped, and the manager will not assign any new containers.

The drain mode takes a node out of service, which can be useful for performing maintenance or, as in this case, testing the ability of a swarm to redistribute its workload. Run the docker service ps exampleapp_mvc command, and you will see how the status of the service has changed.

```
ID              NAME                      NODE      DESIRED STATE   CURRENT STATE
7jd1yop74mxfy   exampleapp_mvcapp.1       worker1   Running         Running
2ejbexg6yezd9   exampleapp_mvcapp.2       worker1   Running         Running
cse2cyutpvxh9    \_ exampleapp_mvcapp.2   worker2   Shutdown        Shutdown
5r9y800jugey8   exampleapp_mvcapp.3       worker1   Running         Running
cktdzf0ypzcpt   exampleapp_mvcapp.4       worker3   Running         Running
6j8h32cikboe2   exampleapp_mvcapp.5       worker3   Running         Running
5esdl2d3jd1ee    \_ exampleapp_mvcapp.5   worker2   Shutdown        Shutdown
```

The manager node responded to the change in the swarm configuration by instructing the worker1 and worker3 nodes to start additional containers. The containers on the drained node are not removed, which means they can be used again once the server is returned to the active state. Run the command shown in Listing 7-29 on the manager node to reactivate the node.

Listing 7-29. Activating a Node

```
docker node update --availability active worker2
```

The manager will not automatically redistribute the containers in a service when you reactivate a node as long as it has been able to achieve the desired state using the remaining nodes in the swarm. Run the command shown in Listing 7-30 on the manager node to force a redistribution of the containers.

Listing 7-30. Forcing Redistribution of Containers

```
docker service update --force exampleapp_mvc
```

Updating a Service

You can update services to deploy new releases of your applications into the swarm. To create a visible change, alter the banner in the Razor view used by the MVC application, as shown in Listing 7-31.

Listing 7-31. Making a Visible Change in the Index.cshtml File in the ExampleApp/Views/Home Folder

```
@model IEnumerable<ExampleApp.Models.Product>
@{
    Layout = null;
}
<!DOCTYPE html>
<html>
<head>
    <meta name="viewport" content="width=device-width" />
    <title>ExampleApp</title>
    <link rel="stylesheet" href="~/lib/bootstrap/dist/css/bootstrap.min.css" />
</head>
<body>
    <div class="m-1 p-1">
        <h4 class="bg-success text-xs-center p-1 text-white">
            Swarm: @ViewBag.Message
        </h4>
        <table class="table table-sm table-striped">
            <thead>
                <tr><th>ID</th><th>Name</th><th>Category</th><th>Price</th></tr>
            </thead>
            <tbody>
                @foreach (var p in Model) {
                    <tr>
                        <td>@p.ProductID</td>
                        <td>@p.Name</td>
                        <td>@p.Category</td>
```

```
                <td>$@p.Price.ToString("F2")</td>
            </tr>

        }
        </tbody>
    </table>
  </div>
</body>
</html>
```

Save the change to the view and run the commands shown in Listing 7-32 in the ExampleApp folder of the manager node to publish the application, update the MVC application image, and push it to the Docker Hub. You may need to authenticate yourself with the Docker Hub before you push the new image. Don't forget to change the name of the image to replace apress with your Docker Hub account.

Listing 7-32. Publishing the MVC Application and Updating the Image

```
dotnet publish --framework netcoreapp1.1 --configuration Release --output dist
docker build . -t apress/exampleapp:swarm-1.1 -f Dockerfile
docker push apress/exampleapp:swarm-1.1
```

I have tagged the image to indicate that this is a later version that the image originally used to create the service. Run the command shown in Listing 7-33 on the manager node to upgrade the containers in the MVC application service so they use the new image.

Listing 7-33. Updating a Service

```
docker service update --image apress/exampleapp:swarm-1.1 exampleapp_mvc
```

The --image argument for the docker service update command is used to change the image for a service. The update is performed by stopping each container in turn, applying the update, and then starting it again before moving to the next container. It will take a moment for Docker to update all the containers. You can keep track of the progress by running the docker service ps exampleapp_mvc command, whose output includes the image that each container in the service is using.

■ **Tip**   If you have a lot of containers to update, you can speed up the process by using the --update-parallelism argument to the docker service update command, specifying the number of containers that should be taken out of service and updated at the same time. Bear in mind, however, that increasing the number of concurrent updates reduces the number of containers that are available to handle user requests.

Once the changes have been rolled out, use a browser to send an HTTP request to the load balancer, which is listening to port 80 on the manager node. You will see the response shown in Figure 7-8, which shows that the updated MVC application has been used to handle the request.

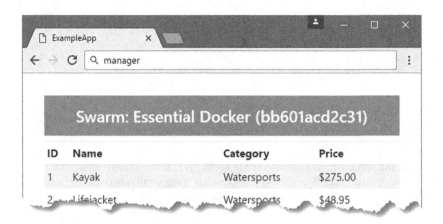

Figure 7-8. *Upgrading a service*

Shutting Down Services

When using a swarm, you stop a service by telling Docker to reduce the number of replicas to zero. Run the command shown in Listing 7-34 on the manager node to scale down the MVC application service so there are no containers running.

Listing 7-34. Scaling Down Docker Services

```
docker service scale exampleapp_mvc=0
```

The Docker workers will stop and remove the containers for the `example_mvcapp` service. It can take a while for all the containers to stop, and you can monitor the process using the `docker service ls` command. Scaling down a service doesn't remove the containers, which Docker keeps in order to speed up the process of scaling up again in the future.

To remove all the components described by the compose file, run the command shown in Listing 7-35 from the `ExampleApp` folder of the manager node.

Listing 7-35. Removing a Docker Stack

```
docker stack rm exampleapp
```

Creating Global Services

The services that I created earlier were replicated, meaning that I specified the number of containers that were required for each service and left the manager node to figure out how to deploy the containers in the swarm.

You can also create global services, in which the service is made up of one container running on each node in the swarm. This can be more predictable than a replicated service because you always know how many containers there are and where they are running, but it provides less flexibility because the number of containers can be increased only by adding additional nodes to the swarm.

■ **Caution**   Don't make the mistake of assuming that global services will let you work around the limitations of stateful applications, such that you can use the load balancer to send all the requests from a single client to the same container. Containers in a global service are still part of the swarm, which means that HTTP requests sent to the ports exposed by the containers are handled using ingress load balancing.

To create a global service, set the `--mode` argument to `global` when using the `docker service create` command or use the `mode` setting in the compose file, as shown in Listing 7-36.

Listing 7-36. Creating a Global Service in the docker-compose-swarm.yml File in the ExampleApp Folder

```
version: "3"

volumes:
  productdata_swarm:

networks:
  backend:

services:

  mysql:
    image: "mysql:8.0.0"
    volumes:
      - productdata_swarm:/var/lib/mysql
    networks:
      - backend
    environment:
      - MYSQL_ROOT_PASSWORD=mysecret
      - bind-address=0.0.0.0
    deploy:
      replicas: 1
      placement:
        constraints:
          - node.hostname == dbhost

  mvc:
    image: "apress/exampleapp:swarm-1.0"
    networks:
      - backend
    environment:
      - DBHOST=mysql
    ports:
      - 3000:80
    deploy:
      mode: global
      placement:
        constraints:
          - node.labels.type == mvc
```

The replicas setting has no effect on a global service: there will be exactly one MVC container running on every node in the swarm that meets the constraints. Run the command in Listing 7-37 from the ExampleApp folder on the manager node to deploy the services described in the compose file.

Listing 7-37. Deploying the Application

```
docker stack deploy --compose-file docker-compose-swarm.yml exampleapp
```

You can see the list of containers by running the command shown in Listing 7-38 on the manager node.

Listing 7-38. Inspecting the Global Service

```
docker service ps exampleapp_mvc
```

The output shows that the containers are running on all three of the nodes that meet the constraint.

```
ID              NAME                  IMAGE                         NODE      STATE
rwq13zt1pmOp    exampleapp_mvc.p4ar   apress/exampleapp:swarm-1.0   worker3   Running
ojfwoezOnyvy    exampleapp_mvc.wn4u   apress/exampleapp:swarm-1.0   worker2   Running
qllo5aOhzy4o    exampleapp_mvc.wked   apress/exampleapp:swarm-1.0   worker1   Running
```

Run the docker service ls command on the manager node to inspect the services and you will see that the mvcapp service is marked as global, like this:

```
ID              NAME                MODE         REPLICAS  IMAGE
7vdsOgsxjxv9    exampleapp_mysql    replicated   1/1       mysql:8.0.0
wd8ouiyu537q    exampleapp_mvc      global       3/3       apress/exampleapp:swarm-1.0
```

Summary

In this chapter, I showed you how to cluster together Linux servers running Docker to form a swarm. I demonstrated how to deploy the example application into the swarm, how swarms load balance requests between the containers they contain, and how to manage the swarm once the application has been deployed. In the next chapter, I explain how to use Docker to create a containerized development environment.

CHAPTER 8

■ ■ ■

Containerized Development

Many of the problems that Docker solves in production also occur during development, especially for large teams working on projects that have multiple components. It can be hard to make sure that every developer has the right version of the tool chain, the runtime libraries, third-party packages, database servers, and schemas and that they are all set up consistently. Add in differences in operating systems and patch levels and it becomes an impossible task.

Using containers for the development environment brings consistency and uniformity to the development process, while still allowing individual developers the freedom to customize their development tools to suit their personal styles. In fact, one of the attractions of a containerized environment is that it standardizes only what is important, without trying to force every developer to work in the same way.

It may seem odd to look at containerized development at the end of a book, but it is only when you understand how the different features fit together that the use of Docker during development can be explained. In this chapter, I show you how to set up a containerized development environment and how to debug an application that is running in a container. Table 8-1 puts containerized development in context.

Table 8-1. *Putting Containerized Development in Context*

Question	Answer
What is it?	Containerized development moves part of the development environment into a Docker container.
Why is it useful?	Containerized development compiles and executes a project using the .NET Core tools running inside a container, which means they will be consistent with the production environment and consistent between developers.
How is it used?	A base image that contains the .NET Core Software Development Kit is used to create an image. A container is created from that image, using a Docker volume to provide access to the project files, which are stored on the host operating system so that they can be put under regular revision control.
Are there any pitfalls or limitations?	Some additional configuration is required to prepare a project for containerization.
Are there any alternatives?	You do not have to containerize development for a project to use Docker to deploy it.

© Adam Freeman 2017
A. Freeman, *Essential Docker for ASP.NET Core MVC*, DOI 10.1007/978-1-4842-2778-7_8

Table 8-2 summarizes the chapter.

Table 8-2. *Chapter Summary*

Problem	Solution	Listing
Build a project in a container	Configure the project to build and run automatically, using a volume to access the project files	1–11
Prepare a project for debugging in a container	Create and run a container that includes the remote debugger	12–17
Debug in a container using Visual Studio 2017	Create an XML configuration file and use it to start the debugger from the command window	18–20
Debug in a container using Visual Studio Code	Configure the debugger using the launch.json file	21, 22

Preparing for This Chapter

This chapter depends on the ExampleApp MVC project created in Chapter 3 and modified in the chapters since. If you don't want to work through the process of creating the example, you can get the project as part of the free source code download that accompanies this book. See apress.com for details.

To ensure that there is no conflict with examples from previous chapters, run the commands shown in Listing 8-1 to remove the Docker containers, networks, and volumes. Ignore any errors or warnings these commands produce.

Listing 8-1. Removing the Docker Components

```
docker rm -f $(docker ps -aq)
docker network rm $(docker network ls -q)
docker volume rm $(docker volume ls -q)
```

Run the commands shown in Listing 8-2 if you are a Linux user and you used your development machine as the manager of a swarm in Chapter 7.

Listing 8-2. Removing the Services and Leaving the Swarm

```
docker stack rm exampleapp
docker swarm leave --force
```

Using Development Mode to Prepare the Database

Previous chapters used a range of techniques to prepare the database for the application, dealing with the need to apply Entity Framework Core migrations and generate seed data.

The situation is simpler in development because there is no production data that can be lost. To that end, modify the Startup class, as shown in Listing 8-3, so that the database is prepared automatically when the application starts in the Development environment.

Listing 8-3. Enabling Database Updates in the Startup.cs File in the ExampleApp Folder

```
...
public void Configure(IApplicationBuilder app,
        IHostingEnvironment env, ILoggerFactory loggerFactory) {

    loggerFactory.AddConsole();
    app.UseDeveloperExceptionPage();
    app.UseStatusCodePages();
    app.UseStaticFiles();
    app.UseMvcWithDefaultRoute();

    if (env.IsDevelopment()) {
        SeedData.EnsurePopulated(app);
    }
}
...
```

Understanding Containerized ASP.NET Core Development

The roles of application and data are reversed when compared to the deployment containers created in earlier chapters. It is the tool chain—the compiler, the runtime, the debugger—that becomes the application and lives inside the container. The data files are the ASP.NET Core MVC project files, which exist outside of the container in a Docker volume. The Docker volume used for development containers uses a folder from the host operating system to provide the contents of a directory inside the container. This is similar to the way that the load balancer configuration file was set up in earlier chapters but uses an entire folder rather than a single file. Figure 8-1 shows how the pieces fit together in a containerized development environment.

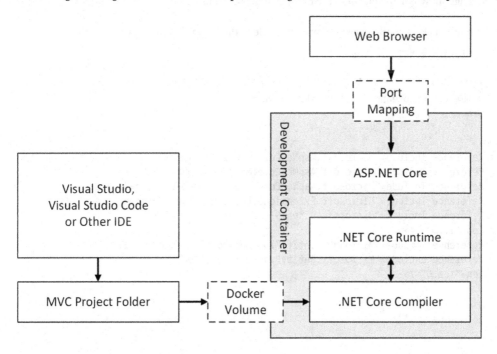

Figure 8-1. *Containerized development*

Using a volume to mount a host folder means that ASP.NET Core MVC project files can be edited using Visual Studio or Visual Studio Code as normal and then compiled inside the development container using the .NET Core compiler. The development container also includes the .NET Core runtime, which can execute the application and expose it for testing through a port mapping to the host operating system. The project files can be managed outside of the container, using regular source code control tools like Git or Subversion, while the tools and execution environment are standardized through the container, whose Docker file can also be placed under version control.

Setting Up Containerized Development

Containerized development is still a relatively new idea and can be a little awkward, especially when it comes to debugging. The quality of tooling for containerized development will improve as containers become more widely used, but for the moment some careful configuration is required to create the development environment and get it working. In the sections that follow, I start by setting up a container for developing and testing an ASP.NET MVC Core application, and then, with a little extra work, I demonstrate how use the Visual Studio and Visual Studio Code debuggers.

Adding the DotNet Watcher Package

The first challenge in setting up a development container is making sure that it reflects the changes that you make to the code files. ASP.NET Core MVC responds immediately when one of its Razor views changes but doesn't detect changes in the C# classes.

The Microsoft.DotNet.Watcher.Tools package is used to monitor a project from inside the container and restart the .NET Core runtime when a file change is detected, ensuring that changes made by the developer are reflected inside the container.

Add the package shown in Listing 8-4 to the ExampleApp.csproj file.

Listing 8-4. Adding a Package in the ExampleApp.csproj File in the ExampleApp Folder

```
<Project Sdk="Microsoft.NET.Sdk.Web">

  <PropertyGroup>
    <TargetFramework>netcoreapp1.1</TargetFramework>
  </PropertyGroup>

  <ItemGroup>
    <PackageReference Include="Microsoft.AspNetCore" Version="1.1.1" />
    <PackageReference Include="Microsoft.AspNetCore.Mvc" Version="1.1.2" />
    <PackageReference Include="Microsoft.AspNetCore.StaticFiles" Version="1.1.1" />
    <PackageReference Include="Microsoft.Extensions.Logging.Debug" Version="1.1.1" />
    <PackageReference Include="Microsoft.VisualStudio.Web.BrowserLink"
        Version="1.1.0" />
    <PackageReference Include="Microsoft.EntityFrameworkCore" Version="1.1.1" />
    <PackageReference Include="Microsoft.EntityFrameworkCore.Tools"
        Version="1.1.0" />
```

```
    <PackageReference Include="Pomelo.EntityFrameworkCore.MySql" Version="1.1.0" />
    <DotNetCliToolReference Include="Microsoft.EntityFrameworkCore.Tools.DotNet"
        Version="1.0.0" />
    <PackageReference Include="Microsoft.Extensions.Configuration.CommandLine"
        Version="1.1.1" />
    <DotNetCliToolReference Include="Microsoft.DotNet.Watcher.Tools"
        Version="1.0.0" />
  </ItemGroup>
</Project>
```

The change adds the version of the DotNet Watcher package that works with version 1.1.1 of .NET Core and ASP.NET Core and that is required for the examples in this book.

CONTAINERIZING A NEW PROJECT

The examples in this chapter show you how to create a containerized development environment for a project that is already in progress, but you can also create a container right at the start of the development process.

To do this, you need to create a project on the host operating system so that there is a csproj file that lists the NuGet packages you need. Once you have the csproj file, you can create and start the container and start adding the C# and Razor files that your project requires.

If you are using Visual Studio, you can use the New Project Wizard to create the project. If you are using Visual Studio Code (or you just prefer working with the command line), then use the following command to create a new project, where the name of the folder in which the command is run is used as the name for the project.

```
dotnet new mvc --language C# --auth None --framework netcoreapp1.1
```

Once the project has been created, open a new command prompt and navigate to the project. Add the DotNet Watcher package as shown in Listing 8-4 and any other packages that you require. You can then follow the process from Listing 8-5 onward.

Once you have a development container up and running, use you IDE to create the data model, controllers, and views that your application requires.

Creating the Development Image and Compose File

It is possible to create a development container using only the Docker command-line tools, but doing so requires careful attention to ensure that the configuration settings required by the development tools are correct. A more reliable approach, and one that helps ensure that all developers are working with the same environment, is to create a Docker file that is used in conjunction with a compose file that includes the volumes, software-defined networks, and any other containers that the application depends on.

Create a file called Dockerfile.dev in the ExampleApp folder and add the command settings shown in Listing 8-5. This Docker file will be used to create the image for development containers.

Listing 8-5. The Contents of the Dockerfile.dev File in the ExampleApp Folder

```
FROM microsoft/aspnetcore-build:1.1.1

COPY node_modules/wait-for-it.sh/bin/wait-for-it /tools/wait-for-it.sh

RUN chmod +x /tools/wait-for-it.sh

ENV DBHOST=dev_mysql WAITHOST=dev_mysql WAITPORT=3306

ENV DOTNET_USE_POLLING_FILE_WATCHER=true

EXPOSE 80/tcp

VOLUME /app

WORKDIR /app

ENTRYPOINT dotnet restore \
  && /tools/wait-for-it.sh $WAITHOST:$WAITPORT --timeout=0 \
  && dotnet watch run --environment=Development
```

The base image for this Docker file is microsoft/aspnetcore-build:1.1.1, which is provided by Microsoft and contains the .NET Core SDK rather than just the runtime contained in the images used in previous chapters. This means the compiler is available, which allows the code to be compiled inside the container.

The contents of the /app folder will be provided using a Docker volume when the container is created and will act as a bridge between the code editing done using the IDE and the .NET Core compiler and runtime inside the container. This is an important difference from the Docker files in earlier chapters, which copied the project files into the /app directory in the container's file system with a COPY command.

■ **Tip**   The DotNet Watcher package requires that the DOTNET_USE_POLLING_FILE_WATCHER environment to be set to true when it is used in a container; otherwise, it won't be able to detect file changes.

Table 8-3 describes all the commands used in the development Docker file.

Table 8-3. *The Commands in the Development Docker File*

Name	Description
FROM	This command specifies the base image, which includes the .NET Core SDK so that the code in the project can be compiled inside the container.
COPY	This command copies the wait-for-it script into the container's file system. Previous examples have copied the file into the /app directory, but /tools is used in this example because any file copied into /app will not be available once the volume that contains the project files is mounted when the container is started.
RUN	This command executes the Linux chmod command so that the wait-for-it script can be executed when the container is started.
ENV	This command sets environment variables in the container. The DBHOST variable sets the name of the database for the Entity Framework Core connection string. The WAITHOST and WAITPORT variables are used by the wait-for-it package to make sure that the database is ready before the .NET Core runtime is started. The DOTNET_USE_POLLING_FILE_WATCHER must be set to true when the Dotnet Watcher package is used in a container.
EXPOSE	This command exposes a port so the application inside the container can receive network requests. In this example, port 80 is exposed so that HTTP requests can be received by the ASP.NET Core Kestrel server.
VOLUME	This command is used to specify that a volume will be used to provide the contents of a specified directory.
WORKDIR	This command sets the working directory for the container. In this example, the working directory is set to /app, which will contain the ASP.NET Core MVC project files.
ENTRYPOINT	This command tells Docker what to execute when the container is started. In this example, the wait-for-it script is used to wait for the MySQL database to be ready to receive connections, and then the DotNet Watcher package is used to start the .NET project in the Development environment.

The next step is to create a Docker Compose file that describes the overall environment required by the application. Create a file called docker-compose-dev.yml in the ExampleApp folder and add the content shown in Listing 8-6.

Listing 8-6. The Contents of the docker-compose-dev.yml File in the ExampleApp Folder

```
version: "3"

volumes:
  productdata:

networks:
  backend:

services:

  mysql:
    image: "mysql:8.0.0"
    volumes:
      - productdata:/var/lib/mysql
```

```
    networks:
      - backend
    environment:
      - MYSQL_ROOT_PASSWORD=mysecret
      - bind-address=0.0.0.0

  mvc:
    build:
      context: .
      dockerfile: Dockerfile.dev
    volumes:
      - .:/app
      - /app/obj
      - /app/bin
      - ~/.nuget:/root/.nuget
      - /root/.nuget/packages/.tools
    ports:
      - 3000:80
    networks:
      - backend
    environment:
      - DBHOST=mysql
      - WAITHOST=mysql
    depends_on:
      - mysql
```

The compose file is similar to the one used for production, with some changes to make development easier. HTTP requests will be received directly by the MVC application through a port mapped to the host operating system, without the use of a load balancer. You can add another software-defined network and a container for the load balancer if you want to re-create the environment from earlier chapters, but for most projects, working directly with the MVC container will be sufficient during development.

The most significant changes in Listing 8-6 are in the volumes section of the mvc service. In earlier chapters, the application was prepared for deployment using the dotnet publish command and then copied into the container's file system using a COPY command in the Docker file. This process isn't suited to development, where you want to see the effect of a code change without having to regenerate the Docker image and create a new container. The first volume entry in the Docker file solves this problem by sharing the local directory with the container and making its contents available for use in the /app folder, where they will be compiled and executed using the development tools in the .NET Core SDK.

```
...
volumes:
  - .:/app
  - /app/obj
  - /app/bin
  - ~/.nuget:/root/.nuget
  - /root/.nuget/packages/.tools
...
```

This means the container must be started in the ExampleApp folder so that the first volume provides the development container with the files it requires.

However, there are platform-specific files added to the `bin` and `obj` folders for the NuGet tooling packages, so the second and third volume entries tell Docker to create new volumes for those directories. Without these entries, the application would work either on the host or in the container but not both.

The second volume setting shares the `.nuget/packages` folder that is found in the current user's home directory.

```
...
volumes:
  - .:/app
  - /app/obj
  - /app/bin
  - ~/.nuget:/root/.nuget
  - /root/.nuget/packages/.tools
...
```

This is the location that is used to store NuGet packages when they are installed using the `dotnet restore` command, and sharing this folder with the container means that the container can use the packages you have installed on the host operating system so that you don't have to use `dotnet restore` each time you create a new development container. The final volumes entry creates a new volume for one of the folders into which NuGet will put the platform-specific files for the NuGet tools packages.

For quick reference, Table 8-4 describes the development-specific settings in the compose file.

Table 8-4. *The Development-Specific Configuration Settings in the Compose File*

Name	Description
ports	This setting maps port 3000 on the host operating system to port 80 within the MVC container. This will allow HTTP requests to be sent directly to the MVC container without needing to use a load balancer.
volumes	This setting is used to provide the development container with access to the project files and allow it to make use of the NuGet packages that have been installed on the host operating system.

Preparing for a Development Session

Ensure that all the NuGet packages required by the application are available on the host operating system by running the command shown in Listing 8-7 in the `ExampleApp` folder.

Listing 8-7. Updating the NuGet Packages

```
dotnet restore
```

Using a Docker volume to share the host operating system's NuGet packages with the development container is a useful technique, but you must ensure that they are up-to-date before you start a development container. The advantage of this approach, however, is that you don't have to restore the NuGet packages inside the container.

Once the package update has completed, run the command shown in Listing 8-8 in the `ExampleApp` folder to process the development compose file and build the image that will be used to create the container that will run the .NET Core development tools and the MVC application.

Listing 8-8. Processing the Development Compose File

```
docker-compose -f docker-compose-dev.yml -p dev build
```

■ **Note**   If you are a Windows or macOS user, you must enable drive sharing, as described in Chapter 5, so that Docker can share the project directory with the container.

The -f argument is used to specify the compose file, without which the production file would be used. The -p argument is used to override the prefix used for the names of the images, containers, and networks that will be created using the compose file. I have specified a prefix of dev, which ensures that I can run the development services without interfering with the production services I created in earlier chapters (which are prefixed with exampleapp_).

■ **Caution**   The commands in the rest of the chapter rely on the dev prefix. If you use a different prefix when you run the docker-compose build command, then you will need to follow through that change everywhere you see a Docker component referred to by a name that starts dev_.

Starting a Development Session

To begin development, run the command shown in Listing 8-9 in the ExampleApp folder to scale up the mvc service.

Listing 8-9. Creating the Development Service

```
docker-compose -f docker-compose-dev.yml -p dev up mvc
```

Docker will process the compose file and follow the depends_on setting to determine that a container for MySQL is required, along with a software-defined network to connect them and a volume to store the database files. All four components will be created, and you will see the following output as Docker does its work and MySQL goes through its first-use initialization process:

```
...
Creating network "dev_backend" with the default driver
Creating volume "dev_productdata" with default driver
Creating dev_mysql_1
Creating dev_mvc_1
Attaching to dev_mvc_1
mvc_1    | wait-for-it.sh: waiting for mysql:3306 without a timeout
mvc_1    | wait-for-it.sh: mysql:3306 is available after 0 seconds
mvc_1    | watch : Started
mvc_1    | Starting ASP.NET...
mvc_1    | Hosting environment: Development
mvc_1    | Content root path: /app
mvc_1    | Now listening on: http://+:80
mvc_1    | Application started. Press Ctrl+C to shut down.
mvc_1    | Application is shutting down...
```

```
mvc_1    | watch : Exited
mvc_1    | watch : File changed: /app/Controllers/HomeController.cs
mvc_1    | watch : Started
mvc_1    | Starting ASP.NET...
mvc_1    | Hosting environment: Development
mvc_1    | Content root path: /app
mvc_1    | Now listening on: http://+:80
mvc_1    | Application started. Press Ctrl+C to shut down.
...
```

The advantage of specifying the name of a service when using the docker-compose up command is that the command prompt will only attach to the containers for the specified service. In this case, that means you will see the messages produced by the MVC container and not the verbose startup from the MySQL container.

Test that the application is running correctly by opening a new browser window and requesting http://localhost:3000, which corresponds to the port mapping configured for the MVC container in the compose file.

Once the application is running, use your IDE to open the example project on the host operating system, just as you have been doing in earlier chapters, and make the change shown in Listing 8-10 to alter the format of the message passed by the Index action method in the Home controller to its view.

Listing 8-10. Changing the Message in the HomeController.cs File in the ExampleApp/Controllers Folder

```csharp
using Microsoft.AspNetCore.Mvc;
using ExampleApp.Models;
using Microsoft.Extensions.Configuration;

namespace ExampleApp.Controllers {
    public class HomeController : Controller {
        private IRepository repository;
        private string message;

        public HomeController(IRepository repo, IConfiguration config) {
            repository = repo;
            message = $"Host ({config["HOSTNAME"]})";
        }

        public IActionResult Index() {
            ViewBag.Message = message;
            return View(repository.Products);
        }
    }
}
```

The changed file is contained within the host operating system folder that has been shared with the MVC container and that is used to provide the contents of the /app directory. The DotNet Watcher package detects the file change and restarts the .NET Core runtime. When the .NET Core runtime starts, it will also detect the changed file and recompile the project, after which the Program class is executed and ASP. NET Core is started. Reload the browser and you will see the changed response shown in Figure 8-2. (The message will be prefixed with Swarm if you are a Linux user and you followed the examples in Chapter 7.)

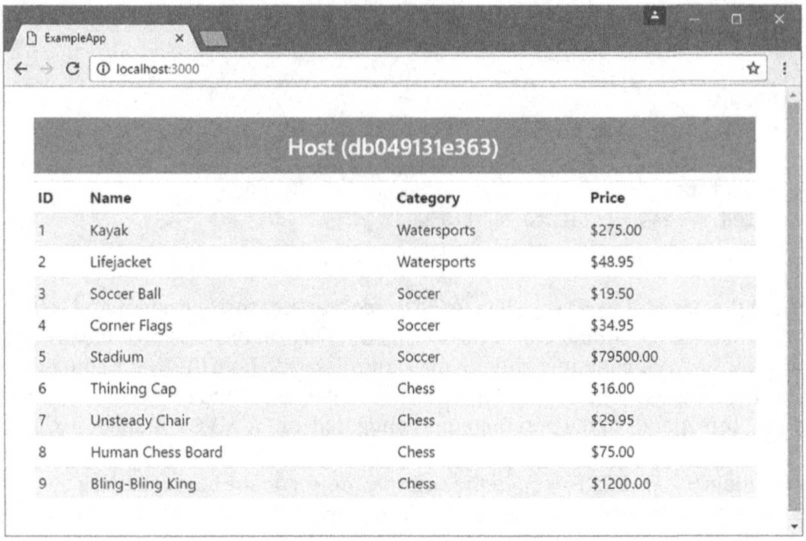

Figure 8-2. Making a change to the example application

■ **Tip**   If you make a change that generates a compiler error, then the details of the problem will be displayed in the output from the development container. The DotNet Watcher package is smart enough to wait until the project compiles without error before starting the ASP.NET Core MVC application again.

When your development session ends, you can type `Control+C` at the command prompt to stop the MVC container, leaving the MySQL container running in the background. If you want to stop all the containers, run the command shown in Listing 8-11 in the ExampleApp folder. The containers are left in place and can be restarted using the command from Listing 8-9.

Listing 8-11. Stopping All Containers

```
docker-compose -f docker-compose-dev.yml -p dev stop
```

Setting Up Container Debugging

Visual Studio and Visual Studio Code can be configured to debug an application running in the container, although the process is a little awkward. The awkwardness arises because the debugger has to run inside the container but must be controlled from outside through the IDE, as shown in Figure 8-3.

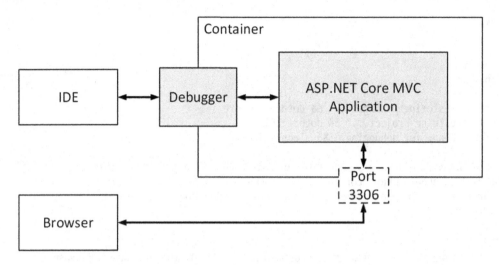

Figure 8-3. *Debugging in containerized development*

In the sections that follow, I describe the process of setting up the debugger in a container and configuring both IDEs to use it.

Creating the Debugging Docker File

The debugger isn't included in the base image used for the development container and must be added in the Docker file. Create a file called Dockerfile.debug in the ExampleApp folder and add the configuration settings shown in Listing 8-12.

Listing 8-12. The Contents of the Dockerfile.debug File in the ExampleApp Folder

```
FROM microsoft/aspnetcore-build:1.1.1

RUN apt-get update && apt-get install -y unzip

WORKDIR /clrdbg

RUN curl -SL \
        https://raw.githubusercontent.com/Microsoft/MIEngine/getclrdbg-release/scripts/GetClrDbg.sh \
        --output GetClrDbg.sh \
    && chmod 700 GetClrDbg.sh \
    && ./GetClrDbg.sh -v latest -l . \
    && rm GetClrDbg.sh
```

```
EXPOSE 80/tcp

VOLUME /app

WORKDIR /app

ENTRYPOINT echo "Restoring packages..." && dotnet restore \
      && echo "Building project..." && dotnet build \
      && echo "Ready for debugging." && sleep infinity
```

The process for installing the debugger involves three steps. First, the apt-get tool is used to install the unzip tool, which will be used to decompress the debugger installer. Next, the curl command is used to download an installation script. Finally, the install script is run and downloads and sets up the debugger in the /clrdbg directory.

■ **Caution**   It is important that you create the Docker file exactly as it is shown in the listing; otherwise, the debugger won't work. If you encounter problems, then use the Docker file included in the source code download for this chapter, which is linked from the apress.com page for this book.

Notice that the ENTRYPOINT command doesn't start the .NET Core runtime or the debugger. The process for debugging in a container is to use the docker exec command to connect to the container once it is running, start the debugger, and then use it to start the application. This means the ENTRYPOINT only needs to prevent the container from stopping, which is done using the sleep infinity command.

Creating the Debugging Service

The next step is to update the development compose file so that it includes a description of the service that will be used for debugging, as shown in Listing 8-13.

Listing 8-13. Describing the Debugging Service in the docker-compose-dev.yml File

```
version: "3"

volumes:
  productdata:

networks:
  backend:

services:

  mysql:
    image: "mysql:8.0.0"
    volumes:
      - productdata:/var/lib/mysql
    networks:
      - backend
    environment:
      - MYSQL_ROOT_PASSWORD=mysecret
      - bind-address=0.0.0.0
```

```
mvc:
  build:
    context: .
    dockerfile: Dockerfile.dev
  volumes:
    - .:/app
    - /app/obj
    - /app/bin
    - ~/.nuget:/root/.nuget
    - /root/.nuget/packages/.tools
  ports:
    - 3000:80
  networks:
    - backend
  environment:
    - DBHOST=mysql
    - WAITHOST=mysql
  depends_on:
    - mysql

debug:
  build:
    context: .
    dockerfile: Dockerfile.debug
  volumes:
    - .:/app
    - /app/obj
    - /app/bin
    - ~/.nuget:/root/.nuget
    - /root/.nuget/packages/.tools
  ports:
    - 3000:80
  networks:
    - backend
  environment:
    - DBHOST=mysql
  depends_on:
    - mysql
```

The debug service is similar to the mvc service but uses the debug Docker file and omits the WAITHOST environment variable used by the wait-for-it package. Save the changes to the compose file and run the command shown in Listing 8-14 in the ExampleApp folder to create the images that will be used for the development services. The RUN commands in the debug Docker file will take a few moments to execute as the installation script and the debugger are downloaded and processed.

Listing 8-14. Building the Development Services

```
docker-compose -f docker-compose-dev.yml -p dev build
```

Starting the Debugging Service

The development and debug containers require access to the same files and use the same port mapping, which means they cannot run at the same time. Run the command shown in Listing 8-15 in the ExampleApp folder to ensure that the regular development container is not running.

Listing 8-15. Stopping the Development Container

```
docker-compose -f docker-compose-dev.yml -p dev stop mvc
```

Once you are sure that the development container has stopped, run the command shown in Listing 8-16 in the ExampleApp folder to start the debugging container.

Listing 8-16. Starting the Debugging Service

```
docker-compose -f docker-compose-dev.yml -p dev up debug
```

The container will start and write out the following message, indicating that it is ready for the debugger to be started:

```
...
debug_1  | Ready for debugging.
...
```

To test the configuration of the container, open another command prompt and run the command shown in Listing 8-17, which tells Docker to start the debugger in the container.

Listing 8-17. Testing the Debugger

```
docker exec -i dev_debug_1 /clrdbg/clrdbg --interpreter=mi
```

The debugger process will start and display the following startup message before waiting for a command:

```
...
=message,text="-----------------------------------------------------------------\n
You may only use the Microsoft .NET Core Debugger (clrdbg) with Visual Studio\nCode, Visual
Studio or Visual Studio for Mac software to help you develop and\ntest your applications.
\n-----------------------------------------------------------------\n",
send-to="output-window"
(gdb)
...
```

The configuration of the IDEs in the following sections allows them to execute the docker exec command to start the debugger and start issuing commands to it, beginning with executing the example ASP.NET Core MVC application. Type Control+C at the command prompt to stop the debugger, leaving the container running and ready for use in the sections that follow.

Debugging with Visual Studio 2017

Visual Studio 2017 includes integrated support for the debugger that is used in containers, but the support is rudimentary and requires rigid adherence to specific Docker files and compose file names and contents, which makes it difficult to use. The approach I use is to take advantage of the debugger support without having to give up control of the Docker configuration.

Create a file called debug_config.xml in the ExampleApp folder, ensuring the contents match those in Listing 8-18.

Listing 8-18. The Contents of the debug_config.xml File in the ExampleApp Folder

```
<?xml version="1.0" encoding="utf-8" ?>
<PipeLaunchOptions
  PipePath="docker"
  PipeArguments="exec -i dev_debug_1 /clrdbg/clrdbg --interpreter=mi"
  TargetArchitecture="x64" MIMode="clrdbg"
  ExePath="dotnet" WorkingDirectory="/app"
  ExeArguments="/app/bin/Debug/netcoreapp1.1/ExampleApp.dll">
</PipeLaunchOptions>
```

This XML file provides the configuration information that will allow Visual Studio to run the command that starts the debugger in the container and send commands to it. The configuration is expressed using the attributes of the PipeLaunchOptions element, which are described in Table 8-5.

Table 8-5. *The Configuration for the Debugger*

Name	Description
PipePath	This is the name of the program that will be run to provide the IDE with a connection to the debugger. For containerized development, this is Docker.
PipeArguments	These are the arguments that are passed to Docker to create the connection to the debugger.
TargetArchitecture	This is the architecture for the platform, which must be set to x64.
MIMode	This setting specifies the machine interface mode, which must be set to clrdbg for containerized development.
ExePath	This is the name of the command that will be run to start the application that will be debugged. For containerized projects, this is dotnet, referring to the .NET Core runtime.
ExeArguments	This is the argument that will be passed to dotnet to start the project and that should be set to the DLL that is produced by the compilation process.
WorkingDirectory	This specifies the working directory for running the application under the debugger.

Open the Visual Studio command window by selecting Other Windows ➤ Command Window from the View menu. The command window allows you to run commands directly in Visual Studio and is required to start the debugger.

Make sure the debugging container is running using the command in Listing 8-16, then enter the command shown in Listing 8-19 into the Visual Studio command window, and finally press Return to start the debugger.

Listing 8-19. Starting the Debugger

```
Debug.MIDebugLaunch /Executable:dotnet /OptionsFile:"C:\ExampleApp\debug_config.xml"
```

When entering the command, set the /OptionsFile argument to the full path to the debug_config.xml file. For me, this file is in the C:\ExampleApp folder, but you must set this value to reflect the location of the file on your system.

Testing the Debugger

The debugger will start and load the files that it needs to execute the ASP.NET Core MVC application. Once the startup process is complete, the standard Visual Studio debugger controls and features are enabled.

To test the debugger, open the HomeController.cs file, right-click the first statement in the Index action method, and select Breakpoint ➤ Insert Breakpoint from the pop-up menu. Open a browser tab and request http://localhost:3000 to send an HTTP request to the application through the container's port mapping. When the handling of the request reaches the breakpoint, the debugger will halt execution of the application and pass control to Visual Studio, as shown in Figure 8-4. You can use the menu items in the Debug menu to control the execution of the application and to inspect the current state.

```
4
5     namespace ExampleApp.Controllers {
6         public class HomeController : Controller {
7             private IRepository repository;
8             private string message;
9
10            public HomeController(IRepository repo, IConfiguration config) {
11                repository = repo;
12                message = $"Host ({config["HOSTNAME"]})";
13            }
14
15            public IActionResult Index() {
16                ViewBag.Message = message;
17                return View(repository.Products);
18            }
19        }
20    }
21
```

Figure 8-4. *Debugging an application in a container using Visual Studio*

Select Debug ➤ Continue to resume execution of the application or Debug ➤ Stop Debugging to bring the debugging session to an end. When you have finished debugging, you can stop the container by typing Control+C in the command prompt you used to start it or by opening another command prompt, navigating to the ExampleApp folder, and running the command shown in Listing 8-20.

Listing 8-20. Stopping the Debugging Container

```
docker-compose -f docker-compose-dev.yml -p dev stop debug
```

Debugging with Visual Studio Code

Open the ExampleApp folder using Visual Studio Code and select Debug from the View menu to open the debugging controls. If you are prompted to add assets to build and debug the project, then click the Yes button.

Click the settings icon, as shown in Figure 8-5, and select .NET Core from the list of options.

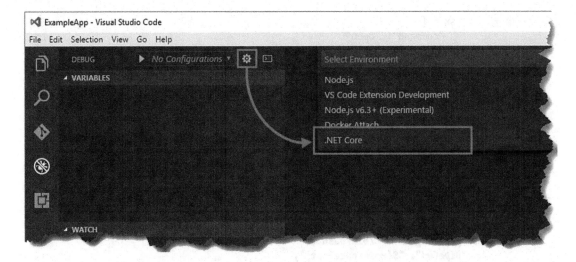

Figure 8-5. *Beginning the debugging configuration*

■ **Note** The example in this section requires the C# extension for Visual Studio Code described in Chapter 3.

Visual Studio Code will create a file called launch.json in a new folder called .vscode, and the file will be opened for editing. Edit the file to make the changes and additions shown in Listing 8-21, which configure Visual Studio Code so that it can run the debugger in the container.

Listing 8-21. Configuring Debugging in the launch.json File in the ExampleApp/.vscode Folder

```
{
    "version": "0.2.0",
    "configurations": [
        {
            "name": ".NET Core Launch (web)",
            "type": "coreclr",
            "request": "launch",
            "preLaunchTask": "build",
```

```
        "program": "/app/bin/Debug/netcoreapp1.1/ExampleApp.dll",
        "args": [],
        "cwd": "/app",
        "stopAtEntry": false,
        "internalConsoleOptions": "openOnSessionStart",
        "launchBrowser": {
            "enabled": false,
            "args": "${auto-detect-url}",
            "windows": {
                "command": "cmd.exe",
                "args": "/C start ${auto-detect-url}"
            },
            "osx": {
                "command": "open"
            },
            "linux": {
                "command": "xdg-open"
            }
        },
        "env": {
            "ASPNETCORE_ENVIRONMENT": "Development"
        },
        "sourceFileMap": {
            "/app": "${workspaceRoot}",
            "/Views": "${workspaceRoot}/Views"
        },
        "pipeTransport": {
            "pipeProgram": "/bin/bash",
            "pipeCwd": "${workspaceRoot}",
            "pipeArgs": ["-c",
                "docker exec -i dev_debug_1 /clrdbg/clrdbg --interpreter=mi"],
            "windows": {
                "pipeProgram":
             "${env.windir}\\System32\\WindowsPowerShell\\v1.0\\powershell.exe",
                "pipeCwd": "${workspaceRoot}",
                "pipeArgs":
                [ "docker exec -i dev_debug_1 /clrdbg/clrdbg --interpreter=mi" ]
            }
        }
    },
    {

        "name": ".NET Core Attach",
        "type": "coreclr",
        "request": "attach",
        "processId": "${command.pickProcess}"
    }
  ]
}
```

■ **Caution**   It is important that you edit the launch.json file so that it precisely matches the listing. If you have problems running the debugger, then try using the project for this chapter that is included with the source code download, which is linked from the apress.com page for this book.

Table 8-6 lists the configuration settings that have been changed or added in the launch.json file and explains what they do.

Table 8-6. *The Debugging Configuration Settings for Visual Studio Code*

Name	Description
program	This setting specifies the path to the DLL that the debugger will use to start the project. The value shown is the default.
cwd	This setting specifies the directory that contains the project files in the container.
launchBrowser:enabled	This setting disables the feature that opens a new browser window automatically when debugging is started.
pipeTransport	This setting denotes the category for configuring the debugger so that it can work with the container.
pipeProgram	This setting specifies the shell that will be used to run Docker.
pipeArgs	This setting specifies the Docker command that will connect to the container and start the debugger.
windows	This section contains the configuration settings for Windows. The individual settings have the same meaning as in the main section, but the values will be used when the debugger is started on Windows machines.

Save the changes to the launch.json file and make sure that the debugging container is running using the command in Listing 8-16. Ensure that .NET Core Launch (web) is selected in the Visual Studio Code Debug drop-down list, and click the green start arrow at the top of the Debug window, as shown in Figure 8-6. If you are prompted to select a task runner, then choose .NET Core from the list and then click the green start arrow to start debugging.

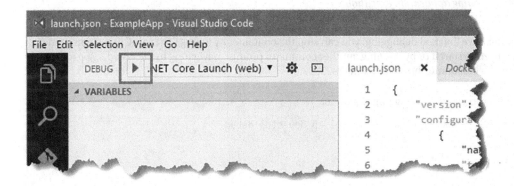

Figure 8-6. *Starting the Visual Studio Code debugger*

165

Testing the Debugger

The debugger will start and load the files that it needs to execute the ASP.NET Core MVC application. Once the startup process is complete, the standard Visual Studio Code debugger controls and features are enabled, just as though you were running the normal built-in debugger.

Select Explorer from the View menu to return to the list of files in the project, open the HomeController.cs file in the Controllers folder, and click at the left edge of the window next to either of the lines of code in the Index method to create a breakpoint, as illustrated by Figure 8-7.

```
13              }
14

            2 references
15              public IActionResult Index() {
●  16                  ViewBag.Message = message;
17                  return View(repository.Products);
18              }
19          }
20      }
21
```

Figure 8-7. *Creating a breakpoint*

Open a new browser window and request the http://localhost:3000 URL, which will target the MVC application running in the debugging container. When the request handling reaches the breakpoint, the debugger will halt execution of the application and pass control to Visual Studio Code. At this point, you can use the normal Visual Studio Code debugging controls to step through the application or inspect the current state.

Click the green button in the debugging control palette, as shown in Figure 8-8, to resume execution of the application.

Figure 8-8. *Resuming application execution*

When you have finished debugging, you can stop the container by typing Control+C in the command prompt you used to start it or by opening another command prompt, navigating to the ExampleApp folder, and running the command shown in Listing 8-22.

Listing 8-22. Stopping the Debugging Container

```
docker-compose -f docker-compose-dev.yml -p dev stop debug
```

Summary

In this chapter, I explained how the Docker features described in earlier chapters can be used to create a containerized development environment, which ensures that all the developers on a project are able to work consistently while still able to use their preferred IDE configuration. I showed you how to set up the development container so that it automatically compiles and runs the application when there is a code change and how to debug a containerized application.

And that is all I have to teach you about the essentials of using Docker for ASP.NET Core MVC applications. I started by creating a simple Docker image and then took you on a tour of the different Docker features including containers, volumes, software defined-networks, composition, swarms, and, finally, containerized development.

I wish you every success in your Docker/ASP.NET Core MVC projects, and I can only hope that you have enjoyed reading this book as much as I enjoyed writing it.

Index

© Adam Freeman 2017
A. Freeman, *Essential Docker for ASP.NET Core MVC*, DOI 10.1007/978-1-4842-2778-7

Get the eBook for only $5!

Why limit yourself?

With most of our titles available in both PDF and ePUB format, you can access your content wherever and however you wish—on your PC, phone, tablet, or reader.

Since you've purchased this print book, we are happy to offer you the eBook for just $5.

To learn more, go to http://www.apress.com/companion or contact support@apress.com.

Apress®

Printed in the United States
By Bookmasters